VOYAGERS TO CALIFORNIA

VOYAGERS TO CALIFORNIA

by

Del Wilcox

Sea Rock Press
Elk, California

Published in the United States of America
by
Sea Rock Press
P.O. Box 58
Elk, California
95432

A Teacher's Guide to Voyagers to California
is available from the publisher.

The drawing of the carrack on the title page
is by courtesy of
The Cabrillo Historical Association

Dedication

To all the optimists who came to California

PREFACE AND ACKNOWLEDGEMENTS

VOYAGERS TO CALIFORNIA came into being over many years. At first it was only a lifelong curiousity about history. After I settled in California, I was amazed at how little residents here knew about their state's past. There seemed to be a need for a book about California's exploration and population. When I retired from my psychiatric practice, I decided to combine my interest in history with another interest, writing.

Many people have helped me to produce this book. I met Raymond Aker when I presumptously called him without introduction. He has been very gracious in reading the text, reviewing the maps about the Spanish explorations and Francis Drake, and making many corrections and suggestions. Also he has allowed me to use his excellent drawings. Harry Kelsey also reviewed that part of the book and gave many valuable comments. Herbert Kohl read the text from the standpoint of educational usefulness and advised and coached me in writing a separate Teacher's Guide. His comments have been enormously productive. Where would I be without the Bancroft Library? That great source of California knowledge provided most of the information and illustrations for the book. Bruce Levene edited the early versions and brought the book into being in a dozen ways with his good-humored competence. Leona Walden did the layout work and collaborated with me in producing the maps. Her expertise has been invaluable. My wife, Prue, read every word, managed to convey a sense of encouragement, and gave many valuable suggestions, without producing any domestic crises. I am grateful to all of these people, as well as many others who helped in the evaluation process and gave information, pictures and technical direction.

—Del Wilcox

Table of Contents

PART II

THE AMERICAN ERA

Maps

INTRODUCTION

California! A state with over 29 million people! Bigger than most countries! Yet one of the last places in the world to be discovered by Europeans. This book attempts to describe the original scene as homeland for the California Indians, then traces the course of exploration and settlement by others.

All of this is surprisingly recent. Columbus, of course, began the process with his discovery of the New World. The Caribbean islands, Mexico, Central America, and South America were explored in the next few decades that followed.

California remained a mysterious place hidden in the territory that stretched on north and west. The Spanish made some attempts in the next century to scan this new possession but found little to encourage investment in the northern lands. After abandoning California for 160 years, another Spanish effort during the late 1700's and early 1800's created the unsuccessful mission system.

The discovery of gold in 1848 changed interest in California from apathy to enthusiasm. New groups of players crowded onto the stage. The modern era of settlement and development began.

I call this book **Voyagers To California**. The earliest visitors to California were mariners. Once the routes from the east were mapped, overland travel into the state became common as well. These people were voyagers, too, in a sense. They came across a vast expanse of land and during the Gold Rush were called Argonauts. The name was taken from the sailors in the Greek fable about Jason's search for the Golden Fleece.

The voyagers are described as history grouped them: explorers, churchmen, soldiers, settlers, people passing through, and others. Some are described easiest by their national or racial origin. How they came was important and I have given separate chapters to sea and overland routes to California. The lives of outstanding individuals highlight the surges of history and I have interlaced the story with brief biographies of memorable persons.

The book is divided into SPAIN AND MEXICO'S ALTA CALIFORNIA and THE AMERICAN ERA to separate the two great periods of ownership and culture in California history. Of course, there are many areas where the two intertangle.

I found it impossible to restrict the time period being covered. The book is not an attempt to give a comprehensive history of the state. It only hopes to describe the arriving strands of people who became Californians. That process of immigration continues to be interesting and dynamic to this day.

PART I
SPAIN AND MEXICO'S
ALTA CALIFORNIA

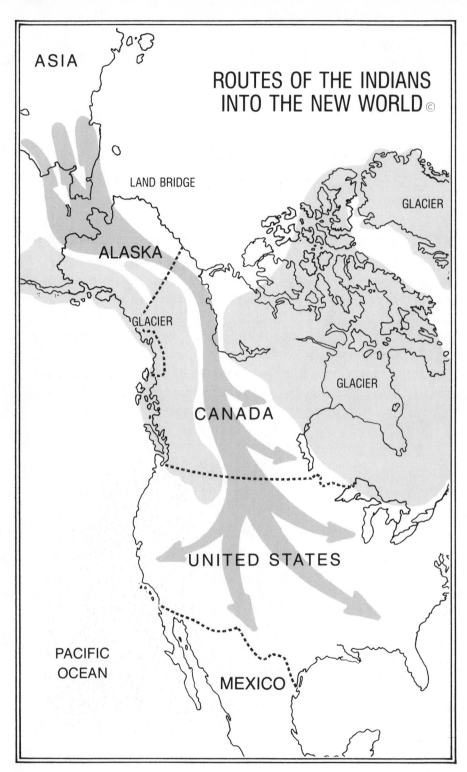

ROUTES OF THE INDIANS
INTO THE NEW WORLD ©

ASIA

LAND BRIDGE

ALASKA

GLACIER

GLACIER

GLACIER

CANADA

UNITED STATES

PACIFIC
OCEAN

MEXICO

CHAPTER 1
THE FIRST TO ARRIVE
THE INDIANS, OUR NATIVE AMERICANS
Ishi

IT IS UNCERTAIN HOW AND WHEN the first people came to California. Almost certainly they came from northeast Asia and were of Mongolian stock. Their body characteristics, including skin coloring, straight black hair, brown eyes, and scant body hair, resemble the Mongols of Asia. Peculiarities of the teeth, including unique shapes of the molars, premolars, and incisors, suggest this connection. Apparently, the first Californians migrated before their cousins in Asia developed their present flat profiles and almond shaped eyes. All North and South American Indians are thought to be derived from small numbers of hunters who followed game animals into the unsettled new world.

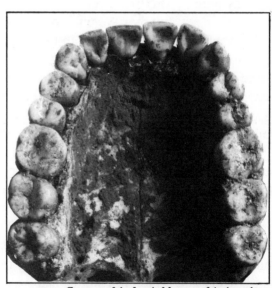

An American Indian skull found near Santa Barbara shows the typical shovel-shaped incisors. The front teeth are shaped on the side toward the tongue in a way similar to that of a shovel. This shape is shared by northeast Asians.

Courtesy of the Lowie Museum of Anthropology,
University of California, Berkeley.

The last Ice Ages locked enormous amounts of polar moisture into vast glaciers. The Bering Sea level fell 300 feet and a land bridge connected Asia and Alaska at least twice, between 32,000-36,000 years ago and 12,000-28,000 years ago. For periods during both of these times the glacier covering all of present-day Canada partially melted, leaving a path of land down the eastern slope of the Canadian Rockies to the present United States. The Indians must have come that way into their new home. Artifacts have been dated by radioactive carbon measurement to as long ago as 25,000-35,000 years past in North and South America. An Indian skull found in Los Angeles has been dated to around 21,600 B.C. California shell mounds, made by these settlers discarding the shells of eaten crustaceans, were started thousands of years ago.

Investigations by anthropologists conclude that probably three distinct migrations from Asia took place. Indians of the Aleut-Eskimo group migrated about 16,000 years ago. Most of the Indians came about 12,000 years ago. About the same time a third group populated the interior of Alaska and the Canadian northwest. Some of these later wanderers may have moved into northern California and the United States southwest as late as 1500 A.D.

There is no reliable evidence that California's first settlers ever found their way here by ship from Asia. Much of their life was oriented to the wealth of the sea, but they were not ocean sailors.

The newly arrived California immigrants found a land of abundant food supply. Although some foraging was ordinary, moving about much to find enough to eat was unnecessary. The consensus of anthropologists is that there were 250,000-300,000 Indians in Alta California when the white man appeared. They were separated into 21 distinct language groups. The northern Indians were marine oriented and lived by gathering seafish, shellfish, acorns, and game. On the Klamath, Eel and Sacramento Rivers the long runs of King salmon were important to the food supply. Around the large inland lakes fish and wildfowl were plentiful.

Acorns were an important food. Oak forests covered much of the north and central parts of the future state. The acorns were gathered in baskets, then soaked in water, to remove the bitter taste made by the tannic acid they contained. The resulting mush was cooked in watertight baskets into which hot stones had been dropped. Acorn mush was a plentiful and nourishing food.

In the mountain foothills a combination of acorn gathering, hunting, and fishing provided life's necessities. To the far south, in the Colorado and Mohave Deserts, mesquite and pinyon nuts supplemented game to make a subsistence living for a few settlers. Along the bottom lands of the Colorado and Kamia Rivers the Indians grew corn, pumpkins and beans. California supported a large population which prospered and lived in harmony with the land and sea.

Except for the Mohave and Yuma Indians there were no tribes similar to those that existed in central and eastern North America. Large group allegiances were unknown. Villages usually contained less than 100 persons, tied together mostly by family and kinship. Rather than great warriors, chiefs were civil authorities, of not great consequence. Wars were usually for revenge, not for acquisition of property or for personal glory.

As befitted the mild weather clothing was scanty. Men wore either nothing or a skin around their middle. Women wore short aprons front and back, fastened at the waist. Moccasins were used in north and cen-

Courtesy of the A.E. Wilder Collections, Kelley House Museum, Mendocino.

A Pomo Indian of Mendocino County weaves a basket at the Big River Rancheria in the 1860's.

tral California. In the southern deserts some tribes wore sandals made from yucca fibers. A skin blanket was worn about the shoulders in bad weather.

Basket weaving was a highly developed art, using grass, willow and other fibers. Some tribes, mostly in the south, made pottery vessels.

A variety of housing was constructed for individual and communal use, using planks, bark, brush and earth. The sweathouse was a common feature of community living. This was a building used daily by men and boys, only as a sort of club. Users lounged about a central fire in a partially excavated building covered with planks and dirt. Sweating helped remove the human smell, an aide in hunting. The community dance house was a larger building used for ceremonial dances and rituals. Smaller teepees were erected for sleeping and nut storage.

Courtesy of the A.E. Wilder Collections, Kelley House Museum, Mendocino.

The sweathouse of the Big River Rancheria in the 1860's.

Different types of boats were built for use on the area's bays, rivers and lakes. These could be dugouts, plank canoes, or tied tule balsa reeds shaped into rafts. Ocean travel was avoided except in the more placid southern California waters. Fishing was done mostly in pools, with nets or using poisonous roots. Only occasionally were fishhooks used. Salmon or sea lions were killed with spears and harpoons. Abalone, mussels, clams and oysters were consumed in great quantities. In the San Francisco Bay region, mounds of these discarded shells existed by the hundreds—some were as large as 600 feet long and 30 feet high. The shells sometimes accumulated over periods of more than 4000 years. Shells were worn as personal ornaments and made into strings of beads for use as money.

Hunting and warfare relied on the use of bows, arrows and spears. Wars often arose because one tribelet believed that a death had been caused by the magic of enemies. Captives taken were sometimes executed.

This civilization proved to be quite stable and, compared to other areas in what became the United States, supported a large population.

The effect of Europeans on this world was disastrous. The Spanish came hoping to find gold and tried to force the Indian culture into a Spanish mold, and convert the residents to Christianity. Instead, the Indian culture was destroyed and the population racked by new diseases. Mission Indians found themselves in bondage. They fought back by trying to desert the missions. The Indians retreated to lands away from the coastal settlements and harrassed the impotent Spanish establishment by waging guerrilla warfare. They had achieved a balance of power with their European adversaries, until the Americans arrived.

American attitudes toward the Indians were malignant. Also, there were a lot more Americans. Centuries of battling the more hostile eastern Indians had produced an implacable hatred. "The only good Indians were dead Indians". Women and children were as undesirable as men. "Mites make lice," the Americans thought, and all Indians had to be scourged. Small incidents produced justification for massacres. California Indians, with their comparatively simple social structure, were held in worse contempt than their eastern relatives. The derisive term, "Digger Indians", was applied to these gatherers of clams and roots. The destruction was devastating and by 1890 the U.S. Census showed only 16,624 Indians in California.

Today the Indians of California continue to find life difficult in their ancestral home. They are wards of the U.S. Government which administers the relationship through the Bureau of Indian Affairs. Indians are now U.S. citizens with the full protection of the law but these rights came slowly. The treaty settling the U.S-Mexican War, which led to California statehood, had guaranteed certain Indian rights. But these rights were never made real because of changes made when the California State Constitution was voted in. Only whites had rights. Indians were made virtual slaves whose labor could be sold to the highest bidder for debts. Their children were often taken from them to be used as slaves. Indians had no rights in court against whites. Lands given to them were taken back as potentially valuable for gold mining.

Indians became people without rights, generally living on the fringes of society, off reservations, subsisting as day laborers for whites. Citizenship rights remained confused although passage of a federal law in 1877 made it possible for Indians to become U.S. citizens. In 1944 the federal government gave $150 to each California Indian for the wrongs that resulted when Congress failed to ratify the Indian treaties of 1851-1852. But Indians still remain wards of the U.S. Government regarding their ownership of property. The state of California provides educational, welfare and health services.

In 1955 the U.S. Government completed a "Roll of California Indians." It numbered over 36,000 persons. Two/thirds were living outside the over 100 reservations and rancherias that exist in the state. California's first settlers remain a troubled minority in American California. Once 100% of the population they are now slightly less than 1% of the Golden State's millions.

Ishi

In August, 1911, an unprecedented event took place near Oroville, California. An Indian man, apparently starving and seaching for food, was found in a slaughterhouse. He seemed totally unacquainted with the ways of civilization. Scientists rushed to the scene and Professor A. L. Kroeber, from the University of California, took charge. This Yahi Indian was literally the last of his tribe. Reporters described him as "the last wild Indian in California." The captive was the last survivor of a band of four who had been rousted from their village in the very wild canyon of Deer Creek by a surveying party in 1908. When this man had been about five years old, about 1865, most of his tribe had been massacred. After this horrible experience the survivors avoided all contacts with whites and existed at a Stone Age level for 40 years.

This was an opportunity to study a man shaped by the patterns of thousands of years, "uncontaminated" by civilization. The man was taken to the Museum of Anthropology at the University where he was giv-

Courtesy of the Bancroft Library, University of California, Berkeley.

Ishi poses as he was in the wild.

en quarters. In a remarkably short time he appeared to be at ease and related comfortably with his new friends and mentors. But he remained evasive about his Indian name. According to Indian belief one's name should be kept secret, a private thing at the center of the soul. It seemed appropriate to name him 'Ishi,' which meant man in his own language.

Ishi never became fluent in English but was able to communicate his thoughts and impressions. He proved to be a remarkable person. Intelligent, dignified, cheerful, he produced a lot of copy for popular writers as well as a bonanza of information for his scientific observers. Ishi demonstrated his skills in hunting, fishing and survival in the wild. Although not eager to return to the wilderness, he didn't object to instructional camping trips. His techniques of making bows, arrows, spears and other Indian necessities were shared with the anthropologists.

*Ishi with his mentor,
A. L. Kroeber,
Professor of Anthropology
at the University of
California, Berkeley.*

*His conformity in dress
has limits. Note his
refusal to wear shoes.*

Courtesy of the Lowie Museum of Anthropology,
University of California, Berkeley.

To a considerable degree Ishi took on the customs and trappings of civilization. Sometimes the results were hilarious, to himself and to his new friends. He learned to eat with our utensils and wore a suit but could never get used to shoes. City entertainments were amusing but a lot of the laughing seemed to be prompted by a wish to be polite. The thing that impressed him most was the number of people in cities. He couldn't remember himself ever seeing more than five people together before. If this new life depressed him, Ishi maintained his cheerful reserve. He knew he was the last of his kind.

The bachelor Indian died in San Francisco in 1916 of pulmonary tuberculosis. Civilization had finally gotten the best of him.

CHAPTER 2
THE NEW WORLD IS DISCOVERED
THE VOYAGES OF COLUMBUS
1492-3, 1493-6, 1498-1500, 1502-4

IMPROVEMENTS IN SHIP DESIGN and navigational instruments made possible the European sea explorations that began in the 15th Century. The Portuguese were the leaders in this. Their ships went down the west coast of Africa, around the Cape of Good Hope at the southern tip of Africa, and finally entered the Indian Ocean. They reached India In 1498; China, Japan and the Spice Islands (present day Indonesia) in 1515. In 1500 a Portuguese mariner accidentally discovered Brazil.

Spain and Portugal were the greatest naval powers in the world. Spain became Portugal's competitor in exploration and tried to catch up. In the process Spain lucked into possession of much of the Western Hemisphere, and with its reluctant backing of Columbus gained most of the wealth.

Columbus, an Italian born in Genoa, had become a master mariner on voyages along the European and African coasts. From a poor family, he was ambitious, intelligent and mostly self-educated. His lifelong fascination was the study of geography.

Columbus became convinced that Cipango (Japan) in the Orient could be reached by sailing west, as well as by sailing south and east around the bottom of Africa as the Portugese were trying to do. Although most educated people of his time believed the earth was round, many also accepted common superstitions. Most sailors thought there were enormous beasts far out to sea, waiting to eat up anyone going there. This meant it was hard to find crewmen willing to sail very far from land.

CHRISTOPH COLVMBVS

Did Christopher Columbus look like this? His first portrait was painted 80 years after his death.

Ancient Greek scholars, Ptolemy and Marinus, had conceived of the world as a sphere. They thought it was about 22,500 miles around, reasonably close to the truth. It was obvious that China and Japan were a great distance east of Europe. Marco Polo had gone overland to China in the 1200's. Were these countries close enough to be reached by sailing west from Europe? Columbus felt certain they were and wanted to lead such a voyage. He consulted the greatest expert of the day, an Italian scientist named Toscanelli, about the estimated distance. Toscanelli thought that Japan was about 4,500 miles from Spain, going west. Always the optimist, Columbus thought the distance was about 3,000 miles. Actually it is 10,000 miles.

Columbus tried to interest King John II of Portugal in the voyage. The king felt Columbus was unrealistic in his enthusiasm for the western route. During these discussions one of Portugal's mariners, Bartholemew Diaz, succeeded in rounding the tip of Africa and sailing into the Indian Ocean. King John decided that he had found his way to the riches of the East and dismissed Columbus. Efforts by Columbus to interest the courts of England and France in his plan also failed.

In 1486 Columbus first proposed his plan to the sovereigns of Spain, King Ferdinand and Queen Isabella. A commission was appointed to study his plan. The commission reported that the Ocean Sea (Atlantic) was too wide for an expedition to Japan to survive the trip. If Columbus did get there, they felt, the curvature of the earth would make him go downhill to Japan and he would never get enough wind to sail back up! Columbus was discouraged but the queen liked him and she appointed a new commission to study the matter. Again, the finding was against him. Many people at Court saw Columbus as a pushy foreigner. The royal couple felt compelled to turn him down a second time. Then, at the last moment, when Columbus was in the process of leaving the Court for good, a wealthy and influential man agreed to help finance the voyage. The sovereigns relented and decided to back the expedition.

A grand bargain was struck between the Court and Columbus. He was made an admiral, and also Viceroy and Governor-General of any lands he discovered. He was allowed to draw up a noble coat of arms. The monarchs told Columbus that he could keep one tenth of all riches found and that part of all taxes levied would be his. These wildly unrealistic pledges were never kept, although Columbus did benefit substantially from the treasures he found. But he resented not receiving the full, promised amounts.

Three ships were provided for the expedition. The *Nina* and the *Pinta* were small, narrow ships called caravels. The flagship, the *Santa Maria*, was somewhat bigger, wider and heavier. The ships were about 70-80 feet long with only a 6-7 foot draft. Each had three masts. The two forward sails were square; the stern sail, called a lateen, was triangular in shape.

Ninety men and boys, including Columbus's brother, left Spain on August 3, 1492. They stopped for needed repairs at the Canary Islands off northwest Africa. Then, on September 6, with fresh supplies and water, the ships sailed west. The sailors were fearful, worried they would never see Spain again. Columbus tried to calm the men by keeping two logs. In the one he allowed them to see, the calculated distances sailed from home were shorter than those marked in the second log (these shorter distances actually turned out to be more accurate).

After a near mutiny, landfall was likely made at the island of Samana Cay near Cuba on October 12. Recently the route of Columbus has been recalculated using computers, giving a more accurate account of wind and current influences as well as speeds on different days. Samana Cay is 65 miles southeast of the island of San Salvadore, before 1986 thought to be the first landing in the New World. They had been at sea only a little more than a month. The Admiral thought they must be near China, although the natives didn't look Oriental.

The ships explored the surrounding sea. Columbus found small islands nearby that he named for the Spanish monarchs. Searching for Japan he discovered present day Cuba and Haiti. On Christmas Day the *Santa Maria* ran aground in Haiti and broke up. Lumber and equipment were salvaged from the ship and a fort erected from the timbers. The loss of his ship was eased by the friendly visit of a local Indian king and the Indians brought gifts of gold in small quantities. Columbus felt that his hopes for finding riches were coming true but since he had only the *Nina* left it was imperative to return to Spain. The *Pinta* had been sailed away by its captain on the trip to Haiti.

Leaving men at the fort Columbus began his voyage back to Spain. After two days at sea the *Pinta* reappeared. The ships returned to Navidad in Haiti. On January 16, 1493 they again set to sea and after a stormy and dangerous voyage the *Nina* and *Pinta* reached Palos, Spain. At the Court in Barcelona Columbus and his crew were given an exuberant welcome. No one was sure what had been found but it seemed completely new and very important. Columbus was given a large award of money for being the first man to find the Indies by sailing west.

The second voyage to the New World was a much more impressive effort. In the fall of 1493 Columbus returned with 17 ships. After only three weeks they reached the island of Dominica, southeast of Haiti. There were skirmishes with the Indians. Returning to Navidad he found that all of his settlers had been killed after fights with the Indians. New settlements were made. An expedition was organized to search for the gold mines rumored to be hidden in the mountains.

While Columbus went off to explore Cuba (which he thought must be connected to the mainland of China) his men brutally mistreated the Indians. Eventually a great battle was fought between Columbus, his forces and 10,000 Haitian Indians, who were terrified of the horses and guns. The Spaniards subdued the Indians, sent many back to Spain as slaves and forced others into slavery to produce gold. But there was little gold in these islands so the Spanish asked the impossible. Torture and murder caused great loss of life in the Indian population; in a few years they were almost wiped out. So, having met with little success in his search for riches, on March 10, 1496, Columbus sailed for Spain to get new orders.

On his third voyage, from 1498 to 1500, Columbus wanted to explore the seas southeast of the island of Hispaniola (present day Haiti and the Dominican Republic). He sailed with six ships, three of which went to Haiti. Columbus sailed south from the Canary Islands to the Cape Verde Islands, then south and east until he had a landfall at the island of Trinidad, just off the northern coast of South America. The next day he sighted what he called Isla Cancte (Holy Island). This is not an island but a part of the mainland of South America, a fact Columbus never realized. When he returned to Haiti Columbus found the settlement in chaos and a revolt against the men he had left in authority. Columbus sent word to Ferdinand and Isabella to send him help.

In 1500 several ships arrived from Spain with a new governor. Columbus and his brother were arrested as incompetent, put in restraining irons and returned to Spain. On board ship Columbus was told that he could remove the irons but he refused. He was determined to show his monarchs what shameful treatment he had received.

In Spain these injustices were recognized and his property in Haiti was restored to him. Columbus also retained his title as Admiral of the Ocean Sea but lost his positions as Viceroy and Governor-General of the Indies.

His last voyage was from 1502 to 1504. Columbus hoped to find a passage allowing him to go through to the Orient. He returned to Haiti, then explored the east coast of Central America, but was unable to find a passage. It was not until 1513 that the first European, Balboa, saw the Pacific Ocean from the New World. Columbus's voyage was plagued by storms that sickened the men and ruined the food. The Indians encountered were murderous. Columbus decided to return to his base in Santo Domingo in Hispaniola.

His ships, the hulls badly damaged from boring worms, were leaking. In desperation Columbus had to beach them in Jamaica. Two of his men volunteered to attempt reaching help in Santo Domingo in canoes fitted

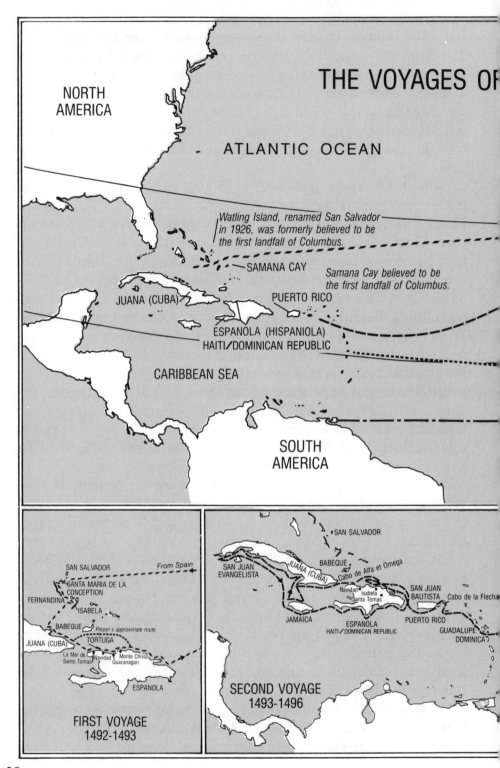

THE VOYAGES OF

NORTH
AMERICA

ATLANTIC OCEAN

*Watling Island, renamed San Salvador
in 1926, was formerly believed to be
the first landfall of Columbus.*

SAMANA CAY

*Samana Cay believed to be
the first landfall of Columbus.*

JUANA (CUBA)

PUERTO RICO

ESPANOLA (HISPANIOLA)
HAITI/DOMINICAN REPUBLIC

CARIBBEAN SEA

SOUTH
AMERICA

SAN SALVADOR
SANTA MARIA DE LA
CONCEPTION
FERNANDINA
ISABELA
BABEQUE *Pinzon's approximate route*
JUANA (CUBA) TORTUGA
La Mar de Navidad Monte Christi
Santo Tomas Guacanagari
ESPANOLA

From Spain

FIRST VOYAGE
1492-1493

SAN SALVADOR
SAN JUAN BABEQUE
EVANGELISTA JUANA (CUBA) Cabo de Alfa et Omega
Navidad Isabela SAN JUAN
Santa Tomas BAUTISTA Cabo de la Flecha
JAMAICA PUERTO RICO
ESPANOLA GUADALUPE
HAITI/DOMINICAN REPUBLIC DOMINICA

SECOND VOYAGE
1493-1496

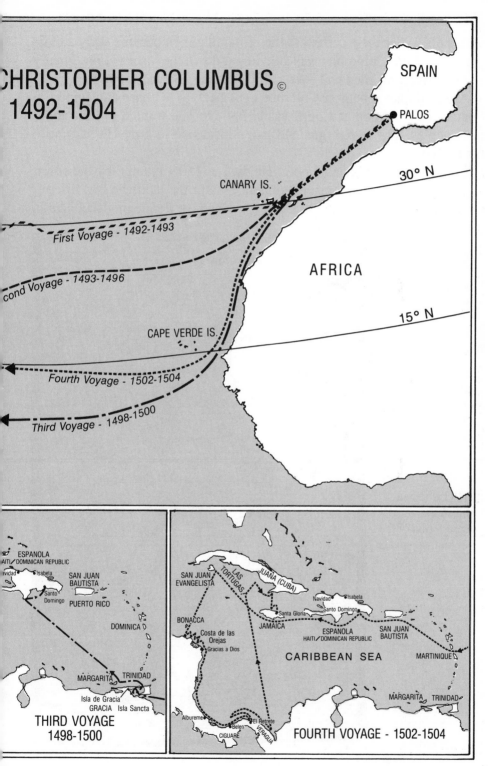

CHRISTOPHER COLUMBUS ©
1492-1504

SPAIN

PALOS

30° N

CANARY IS.

First Voyage - 1492-1493

cond Voyage - 1493-1496

AFRICA

15° N

CAPE VERDE IS.

Fourth Voyage - 1502-1504

Third Voyage - 1498-1500

Third Voyage inset:

ESPANOLA
HAITI / DOMINICAN REPUBLIC
Navidad   Isabela
Santo Domingo
SAN JUAN BAUTISTA
PUERTO RICO
DOMINICA
MARGARITA   TRINIDAD
Isla de Gracia
GRACIA   Isla Sancta

THIRD VOYAGE
1498-1500

Fourth Voyage inset:

SAN JUAN EVANGELISTA
LAS TORTUGAS
JUANA (CUBA)
BONACCA
Costa de las Orejas
Gracias a Dios
JAMAICA
Santa Gloria
Navidad   Isabela
Santo Domingo
ESPANOLA
HAITI / DOMINICAN REPUBLIC
SAN JUAN BAUTISTA
MARTINIQUE
CARIBBEAN SEA
MARGARITA   TRINIDAD
Albureme
Belen   El Retrete
CIGUARE   VERAGUA

FOURTH VOYAGE - 1502-1504

with sails. After their departure the remaining men became surly and finally mutinied. Columbus was able to put down the insurrection. Finally a ship arrived-his men had successfully reached Santo Domingo.

After another rebellion Columbus got back to his base and finally to Spain. His reception at Court was chilly. No one wanted to hear about his troubles. The sovereigns had lost confidence in him. He had made his last voyage.

Columbus never became poor. He died in 1506, ignored by the court, convinced that he was misunderstood, certain the lands he had discovered must be a part of the Orient. It remained for Ferdinand Magellan, a

1493 woodcut illustrates a description of the Columbus voyage.

A woodcut from a publication of Columbus's letter describing his first voyage.

Courtesy New York Public Library.

Portuguese working for Spain, who sailed the first voyage around the world (1519-1522), to show that the New World was between Europe and Asia.

Columbus occupies a supreme position in the history of world exploration. Although a vain, proud, cruel and grasping man, he was also scholarly, courageous, remarkably self-sufficient, and a magnificient sailor. The great man didn't reach California but he tried. His efforts paved the way for others to make the journey in the following decades.

A sinister portrait of Captain Hernando Cortes

CHAPTER 3
THE BEGINNINGS OF CALIFORNIA EXPLORATION
Captain Hernando Cortes
and
Viceroy Antonio de Mendosa

FOR SEVERAL YEARS nothing of great material value came to Spain from the discoveries of Columbus. The newly found islands had few treasures that could be brought back to Spain, as they contained little gold and silver. But because of an adventurer named Hernando Cortes that condition soon changed.

The usual prelude to exploration was to get the backing of rich and powerful persons, have the blessing of the king, and then see what could be stolen from the natives. This required courage as well as leadership and cunning. The risks were great but the rewards could be high. And one could not be squeamish about the methods.

Cortes, a young army captain employed by the governor of Cuba, fit the pattern and he was hired to lead an expedition from Cuba to explore the east coast of Mexico. With a fleet of eleven ships, about 600 soldiers, 16 horses, and a few cannons, Cortes landed in 1519 near the present site of Vera Cruz, Mexico, where a small city was established.

Mexico was dominated by the cruel yet highly developed Aztec Indians. Their capital city, Tenochtitilan, high in the mountains of central Mexico, was located at present day Mexico City. 200,000 Aztecs lived in Tenochtitilan and it was larger than any city in Spain.

The powerful and ruthless Aztecs were hated by other Indian tribes of Mexico, whom they ruled and enslaved. Human sacrifice was a part of their religion. Priests cut out the hearts of slaves offered up to the Aztec gods.

But despite their strength and fierceness the Aztecs were soon intimidated by the tiny Spanish army. They had never seen anything like the

An Aztec drawing shows the Aztecs and Spaniards fighting.

conquistadors' horses, guns, or armor. Thinking Cortes was a god descended from the Sun, the Aztec emperor, Montezuma, sent his ambassadors with gifts for the white visitors. Golden necklaces, discs of gold and silver as big as cartwheels, masks made of precious stones, beautiful clothing, and materials made from brilliant feathers were given to the Spaniards. Cortes was bedazzled and he decided to possess the source of these treasures. For a brief time, to allay Montezuma's suspicions, he showed no signs of this ambition but soon the glittering wealth became an undeniable attraction. Eventually, Cortes attacked Montezuma's forces.

The Spanish captain was advised by a beautiful Indian girl who spoke both the Mayan and Aztec languages. Given to Cortes as a slave, she had a son by him.

The conquistadors divided their Indian adversaries as they advanced toward Tenochtitlan. Battles were fought with the Aztecs and other Indian tribes. The Spanish were courageous and skilled soldiers and their guns and horses were more than a match for the Indians. They were helped greatly when the Tlaxcalan Indians sided with them against Montezuma.

A great battle with the Aztecs was fought near Cholula near the temple of Quetzalcoatl. Cortes and his Indian allies killed thousands of Montezuma's army, whose only weapons were clubs, spears and bows.

Cortes marched into the capital and was met by the Indian emperor in a gracious exchange. Later Cortes made Montezuma his prisoner.

The loot was enormous. Cortes never paid the governor of Cuba for the expense of the expedition. He personally kept 20% of the spoils for himself, as much as he sent the King of Spain.

The governor of Cuba was furious and sent an army to take Cortes prisoner. Cortes fought and defeated them. Then the Indians in Tenochtitlan mounted an insurrection and temporarily banished the Spanish from the city. Cortes recaptured the city in 1521 and during the fighting Montezuma was killed by his own subjects. Cortes became the most powerful man in Mexico.

After his first great successes the fortunes of Cortes gradually declined. King Charles V of Spain feared the conquistador's power and independence but avoided a direct confrontation with him.

Looking for new treasure, rumors of pearls in the Pacific Ocean, called the South Sea, came to Cortes and he decided to explore the west coast of Mexico. Two ships were built. In one ship Fortun Jiminez discovered Baja California, Mexican California, in 1533. Cortes himself went there in 1535 but found nothing of great value.

King Charles V decided that a personal representative was needed in New Spain to look after his interests and he sent his first viceroy, Antonio de Mendosa, who arrived in 1535. Mendosa became the supreme administrator in Mexico. Eased out of power, Cortes returned to Spain in 1540, where he died in 1547. An unadmired figure in Mexico, there is not a statue in his memory anywhere in that country.

Viceroy Mendosa took up the quest for riches and in 1539 he sent out two expeditions. Francisco Ulloa was dispatched to chart the eastern and western shores of Baja California and Francisco Coronado was outfitted with an army to find the fabulous 'seven cities of silver' to the north. Coronado wandered through northern Mexico, New Mexico and as far north as Kansas before straggling home empty-handed.

Meanwhile, great deposits of silver and gold had been discovered in Peru. The Inca empire was subdued by the Pizarro brothers, Diego de Almagro, and their armies. As another great Indian civilization was pillaged with cruelty, unheard of wealth came to King Charles V of Spain.

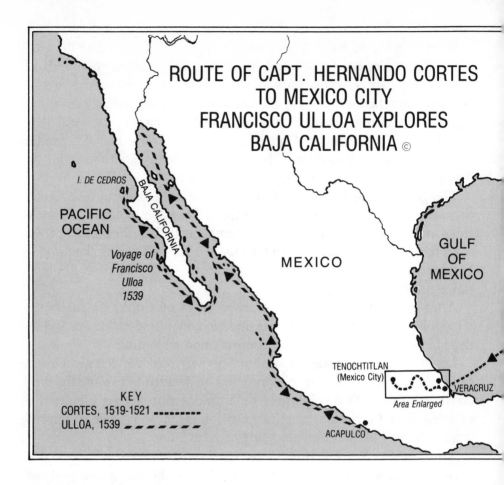

ROUTE OF CAPT. HERNANDO CORTES
TO MEXICO CITY
FRANCISCO ULLOA EXPLORES
BAJA CALIFORNIA ©

I. DE CEDROS

PACIFIC
OCEAN

BAJA CALIFORNIA

Voyage of
Francisco
Ulloa
1539

MEXICO

GULF
OF
MEXICO

TENOCHTITLAN
(Mexico City)

VERACRUZ

Area Enlarged

KEY
CORTES, 1519-1521 ▪▪▪▪▪▪▪▪
ULLOA, 1539 ▬ ▬ ▬ ▬ ▬

ACAPULCO

It is thought that Mendosa had a private agreement with King Charles that allowed him to keep part of any treasure found in Mexico. Although Coronado's search for riches had been unsuccessful perhaps new gold and silver could be found to the north. In 1542 Mendosa organized a naval expedition to explore what became known as Alta California.

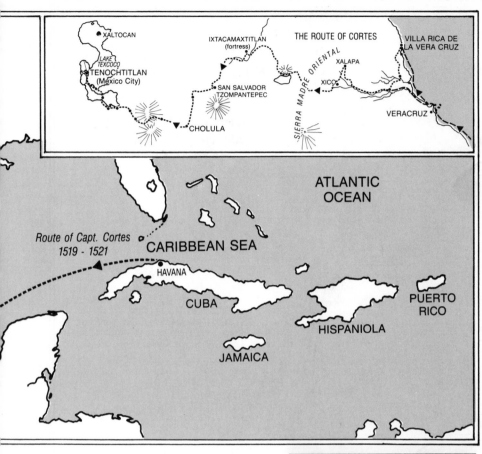

THE ROUTE OF CORTES

XALTOCAN
IXTACAMAXTITLAN (fortress)
VILLA RICA DE LA VERA CRUZ
LAKE TEXCOCO
TENOCHTITLAN (Mexico City)
SAN SALVADOR TZOMPANTEPEC
SIERRA MADRE ORIENTAL
XALAPA
XICO
CHOLULA
VERACRUZ

ATLANTIC OCEAN

CARIBBEAN SEA

Route of Capt. Cortes 1519 - 1521

HAVANA
CUBA
HISPANIOLA
PUERTO RICO
JAMAICA

Viceroy Antonio De Mendosa

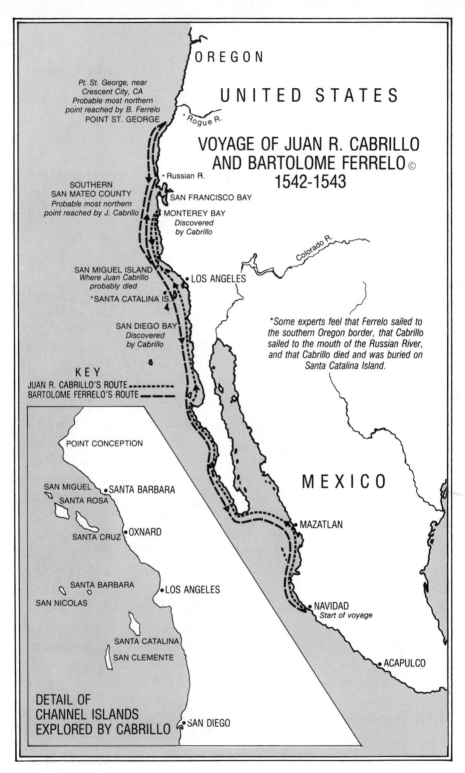

OREGON

UNITED STATES

Pt. St. George, near
Crescent City, CA
Probable most northern
point reached by B. Ferrelo
POINT ST. GEORGE

VOYAGE OF JUAN R. CABRILLO
AND BARTOLOME FERRELO ©
1542-1543

• Rogue R.

• Russian R.

SAN FRANCISCO BAY

SOUTHERN
SAN MATEO COUNTY
Probable most northern
point reached by J. Cabrillo

MONTEREY BAY
Discovered
by Cabrillo

Colorado R.

SAN MIGUEL ISLAND
Where Juan Cabrillo
probably died

• LOS ANGELES

*SANTA CATALINA IS.

SAN DIEGO BAY
Discovered
by Cabrillo

*Some experts feel that Ferrelo sailed to
the southern Oregon border, that Cabrillo
sailed to the mouth of the Russian River,
and that Cabrillo died and was buried on
Santa Catalina Island.

KEY
JUAN R. CABRILLO'S ROUTE ----------
BARTOLOME FERRELO'S ROUTE ━ ━ ━

POINT CONCEPTION

MEXICO

SAN MIGUEL   • SANTA BARBARA
SANTA ROSA

SANTA CRUZ • OXNARD

MAZATLAN

SANTA BARBARA   • LOS ANGELES
SAN NICOLAS

SANTA CATALINA
SAN CLEMENTE

NAVIDAD
Start of voyage

• ACAPULCO

DETAIL OF
CHANNEL ISLANDS
EXPLORED BY CABRILLO   • SAN DIEGO

CHAPTER 4
ALTA CALIFORNIA IS DISCOVERED
The Voyage of Juan Rodriguez Cabrillo
1542-1543

THE MAN VICEROY MENDOSA SENT NORTH was Juan Rodriguez Cabrillo. His voyage was paired with another expedition led by Ruy Lopez de Villalobos, who was to sail due west to the Spice Islands. Information about the geography of the Pacific was so erroneous that it was thought that the two fleets could meet in China. Geographers believed that Japan lay off the California coast, and that North America and Asia were probably joined not too far away in China. The distances involved were greatly underestimated. Villalobos reached the Philippine Islands, which he claimed for Spain, but he could not find a way to get back to Mexico. Cabrillo found Alta California, our American California.

The viceroy hoped the expedition would answer another important question-did the Strait of Anian, the supposed Northwest Passage from the Atlantic Ocean to the Pacific Ocean, exist?. That would be an unhappy discovery for the Spaniards, as it would give other nations access to Spanish domains. Cabrillo was to look for the Pacific opening of the strait.

Like most of the voyages of exploration during that period there were associated commercial aspects. Sources of gold and silver might be found. The new lands were searched for important rivers and straits and possible sites for new settlements. Trade goods were taken along. And, as always with the Spanish, converting the natives to Christianity was an additional reason for glory.

Cabrillo is credited with discovering Alta California. This honor must be shared with his second-in-command, Bartolome Ferrelo, since Cabrillo died on the voyage and Ferrelo completed it.

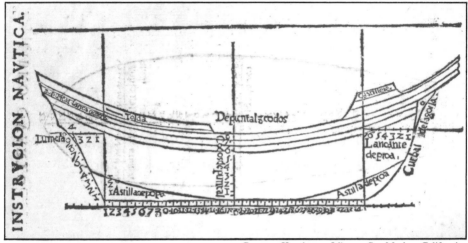

Courtesy Huntington Library, San Marino, California

Method of computing the proportions of a ship's hull
in a Guatemalan shipyard such as Cabrillo supervised.

Recent research has furnished much information about Juan Rodgiguez Cabrillo, but there are still questions about his true origin. Historians have accepted that he was Portugese, but this is not conclusive as no one has been able to find his birthplace. Cabrillo is not a Portugese name. He used the name Juan Rodriguez until his 30's then apparently added the name Cabrillo to distinguish himself from the many other men named Juan Rodriguez in New Spain. He may well have been Spanish.

Most likely, Cabrillo was born into a poor family around 1498-1500 and came to New Spain about age 12 as a kind of apprentice soldier. He fought in Cuba, became a military leader serving Cortes in the conquest of Mexico, then captained a company of crossbowmen in the conquest of Guatemala. He could read and write, manage accounts and conduct business affairs, skills unusual for one of his background. His military efforts were rewarded with grants of property, and these estates and gold mines made him wealthy.

In his younger years he had learned to be an expert sailor, and in Guatemala he built boats and managed a shipyard. He was also something of a journalist, having written an account of a devastating earthquake in Guatemala in 1541, the first private report of an important event in New Spain.

Cabrillo went back to Spain for awhile, found a wife near Seville, then returned to New Spain, where several children were born.

So Viceroy Mendosa persuaded this wealthy, influential and unusual man to take on a new task. Cabrillo had mixed feelings about it all. He complained about an earlier planned voyage that had been cancelled after the leader was killed fighting Indians: "Because he kept begging and pestering me, I came with him in the armada as captain of my own ship and almirante of the armada." No doubt he hoped to make some money as well as serve the crown. His flagship, the San Salvadore, was his personal property. Cabrillo was then in his mid-forties.

Indians pan for gold in Guatemala as they did on Cabrillo's estate.

The three ships used for the voyage, together with those of Villalobos, were from a fleet of 13 ships built in Guatemala. The largest, the *San Salvadore*, was perhaps 100 tons, about 70 feet long and 20 feet wide, with a half deck astern and a low forecastle. The second was the *La Victoria*. The third, a much smaller launch, the *San Miguel*, was abandoned when it became unseaworthy. The 100 or more men who began the voyage consisted of four officers, 25 crewmen, 25 soldiers, black slaves, Indian laborers, merchants, clerks, servants and a priest. One of Cabrillo's sons said in 1560 that his father took along horses, servants, and arms for his own use.

The log of the voyage has not been found. Charts and maps made by Spanish explorers were placed on a master chart in Spain. Then, because it was feared they might fall into the hands of other nations, the originals were destroyed. There does exist an account of the voyage which until recently was attributed to a later historian named Juan Paez. But most likely it was written by a notary public, an official of the state who wrote summaries of such voyages by examining the ship's records and interviewing the survivors. The first part of the report may have been taken directly from Cabrillo's records. Historians believe this was probably then abbreviated by a later explorer, Andres de Urdaneta, when planning his own voyage to the Spice Islands. Urdaneta saved what he found useful and left what we have, which is thought to be in his own handwriting.

Fixing places the expedition visited is difficult today. Almost all the territory was completely new to Europeans. Crude navigational instru-

The known West Coast of Mexico prior to Cabrillo's expedition.

Huntington Library, San Marino, California.

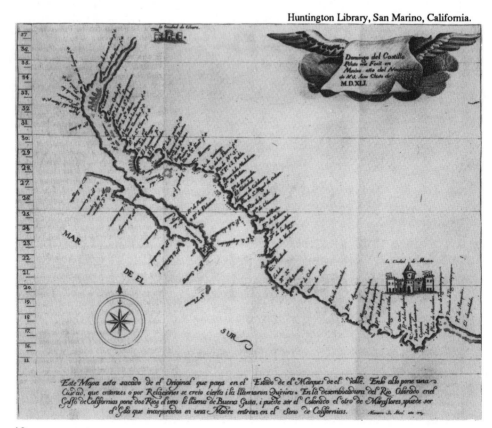

42

ments often made locations difficult to determine. No Spaniard revisited the sites for many years; when settlement finally took place every island, bay, and beach was renamed. Accordingly, there is much room for argument by historians as to Cabrillo's exact route. He is credited with discovering San Diego Bay and Monterey Bay. His chief pilot completed the voyage by sailing farther north, perhaps to Cape Mendocino or southern Oregon.

The ships departed La Navidad (now a tiny Mexican port near Colima on the mainland just south of the tip of Baja California) on June 27, 1542. The strategy was to cautiously follow the coast north, keeping safely offshore except for occasional visits to land.

The first weeks were quite uneventful. The Gulf of California was crossed to the west coast of Lower California. Winds were contrary, but the ships were able to make headway up the sandy, arid coast. The rocky shoals were charted.

Inland were mountains 'high and rough.' Indians were first encountered on August 11th. Then the sailors began to see Indians in greater numbers, with whom they tried to communicate using gestures. On September 27th the Los Coronados Islands were described, San Diego Bay the next day. The coastal latitude was estimated as 34° 40' north, inhabited by Indians with fine canoes. The Indians said there were Spaniards in the interior, which Cabrillo thought to be fanciful tales. That night a landing party went ashore for food. Hostile Indians wounded three of the men.

In the following two weeks the expedition visited San Clemente Island, Santa Catalina Island, and the northern Santa Barbara Channel Islands. Indians continued telling of bearded Spaniards inland. Captain Cabrillo decided to send two crew members to investigate but changed his mind and sent a message through the natives. Of course, he never received a reply.

The ships sailed north probably to present southern San Mateo County. November had brought bad weather, which forced them to return south, where they discovered Monterey Bay. The report says that "Thursday the 16th of November the dawn found them in a large bay made by a turn in the coast...This cove was at 39° and covered with pines down to the sea, so they called it the Bay of Pines." Two days later it continues:"all this coast is very rough, and there is a large near-shore swell and the land is very high; there are mountains that appear to reach to heaven, and the sea beats against them. When sailing near the land, it appears that they are about to fall on the ships. The peaks are covered with snow, therefore we call them the Sierra Nevadas."

The expedition sailed farther south to spend the worst of the winter at what is now San Miguel Island. The Indians were hostile and never stopped fighting the Spaniards. On Christmas Eve sailors went ashore for water and were attacked. A call for help brought Captain Cabrillo leading a rescue party. Going ashore he slipped and 'splintered a shinbone.' Another account says he broke an arm. Possibly both were true, although an eyewitness said his leg was broken. The leg became gangrenous. Cabrillo put his records in order and gave command of the expedition to his chief pilot, Bartolome Ferrelo, a Portugese. About 10 days after the injury Cabrillo died.

The new commander tried to complete the objectives of the voyage and again sailed north. Stormy weather continued in January and February. The weather may well have been more severe than it is now, as a colder world climate seems to have been prevalent then, making snow on the coastal mountains possible.

The explorers worked their way north. At times the ships seemed ready to capsize. The report states they went as far north as 44°, which would be halfway up the Oregon coast. Experts think this is in error, that the ships only sailed close to the vicinity of Pt. St. George near Crescent City. Logs and debris in the water indicated they were sailing off the mouth of a big river.

Exhausted and low on provisions, Ferrelo turned south to sail through more bad weather. The two ships were separated for a time but eventually both returned to La Navidad, on April 14, 1543. The voyage had lasted more than nine months.

The news they brought back received a mixed reception in official circles. No new riches had been found. The northern California coast was forbidding, rocky, and dangerous. The Indians had nothing of value for profitable trade. China or Japan had not been reached, although the sailors believed they had come close. Cabrillo had lost his life, as had Villalobos.

On the other hand, what the explorers did find was reassuring. No Strait of Anian or Northwest Passage had been discovered, denying other Europeans easy access to the Pacific Ocean. The west coast of New Spain seemed secure from invasion by England or France.

Juan Rodriguez Cabrillo emerges as a capable and courageous man. Although he died without recognizing the importance of the discovery of Alta California, neither did the authorities in Mexico, as more than fifteen years passed until the report of his voyage was taken to Spain.

CHAPTER 5
Francis Drake Visits California
1579

AS SPAIN TOOK THE SILVER AND GOLD from New Spain, England was emerging as a maritime power. English privateers entered the slave trade to the New World, seeking to trade with the Spanish settlements there.

In the 1560s the Hawkins brothers, John and William, made voyages hoping to intrude into this Spanish trade. Francis Drake was related to them. The oldest of 12 sons, and apprenticed as a seaman in childhood, Drake was bright and ambitious. He had little formal education yet learned to read and write. In time he earned his own command of a ship and began to sail on the Hawkins' enterprises.

In 1569 Drake went on a slave-trading voyage to Africa and to the Caribbean, commanding a ship in the fleet of Sir John Hawkins . The English felt they had permission to trade but were attacked by Spanish warships. In the battle the English force lost 300 of its 400 men and about 1,000 of its 1,300 tons of shipping. The Hawkins had scant financial loss, however, because they had already traded for considerable amounts of gold, silver, and pearls.

Drake's reputation as a privateer grew when he made other voyages to the Spanish Main in 1570, 1571 and 1572-3, to seize Spanish treasure in reprisal. Drake was rich enough to build his own ship, The Pelican.

Then a new and more audacious voyage was planned by Drake. The Portuguese, Ferdinand Magellan, had circumnavigated the globe for Spain in 1519-22, going west. He discovered the passage (now named for him) from the Atlantic Ocean to the Pacific Ocean at the southern tip of South America. Drake and a group of businessmen, nobles, and privateers decided to enter the Pacific through Magellan's strait and surprise the Spanish treasure ships there. These ships took gold and silver from Spanish colonies in South America to Panama, where it was

Sir Francis Drake
Courtesy of Bancroft Library, University of California, Berkeley

carried overland to be reloaded on ships on the Atlantic side, then sent to Spain. Since they had never encountered any opposition, the Spanish galleons on the Pacific were unarmed.

The details of Drake's voyage were kept secret to avoid unnecessary antagonism by the Spanish crown. How much Queen Elizabeth I knew about the scheme is unknown but it is fairly certain she was a financial supporter.

Besides loot it was hoped that the western opening of the Strait of Anian, or Northwest Passage, would be found. New lands might also be discovered and claimed.   The fleet of five ships was outfitted in first-class style. Drake commanded the largest ship, the *Pelican*, about 100-150 tons and perhaps 80 feet long. The other ships were the *Elizabeth*, *Marigold*, *Swan*, and *Christopher*. The *Pelican* had 18 pieces of artillery and a forge for making repairs. It was a floating arsenal. The crews totalled about 160 men including several boys. There were shoemakers, a pharmacist, a tailor, some musicians, a preacher, and approximately ten "gentlemen". The gentlemen were young upper-class men who went on the journey for adventure and to make a name for themselves.

Drake liked to eat off silver dishes and to be serenaded by the musicians. His cousin went with him and they often painted watercolors in the ship's log of the coasts and the flora and fauna. Drake also liked to preach on Sundays. He was said to be a stern man but of good humor and easily approached. At the time of the voyage he was in his mid-thirties.

They left from Plymouth on December 3, 1577. Drake had three books on navigation and a special five foot map of the world, made up for him in Portugal. This had the best information known at the time. World geography was so poorly understood that voyagers always hoped to find a pilot, someone who had been there before, to give advice and directions.

The ships made a rendezvous in Morocco, then captured a Portuguese ship in the Cape Verde Islands off Africa. The master of the ship was held as a pilot since he knew the Brazilian coast. Then they crossed the Alantic and went down the coast of Brazil and Argentina, wintering at Port San Julian, where Magellan had stayed 58 years before.

Quarrels broke out between the crew and the gentlemen. The exact nature of the dispute is difficult to determine from the accounts written by survivors. Drake feared that one of the gentlemen , Thomas Doughty, was treacherous and inciting mutiny. Doughty was found guilty at a trial and executed.

Drake's little flotilla headed for the Straits in August. There were now only three ships left; the others hadn't proved seaworthy and were abandoned. When the *Pelican* entered the Straits Drake renamed it *The Golden Hind*, in honor of one of his patrons.

Passage through the Straits of Magellan was made in sixteen days, a remarkably short time. The *Marigold* then soon disappeared in a terrible storm. Drake's ship, driven south by fierce winds, became separated from the *Elizabeth*, which returned to England. During this terrible weather the ship was blown south to Cape Horn. The open water between Cape Horn and Antartica is named Drake Passage.

Finally, Drake made headway north. He landed on the island of Mocha, where Indians attacked the shore party. Two of his men were killed and Drake was wounded in the face by an arrow.

At the Spanish city of Valparaiso, in present day Chile, he raided a ship and took gold, wine and, of greater importance, the ship's pilot and

Courtesy Raymond Aker.

Raymond Aker's rendering of the Golden Hind and an accompanying bark in California waters. The fate of the bark is not known.

charts. At 30 degrees south latitude a watering party was set upon by the Spanish. One of his men was killed. At 19 degrees south latitude he raided another Spanish ship, capturing some silver and coins.

At Callao, the port of Lima, Peru, Drake found several ships but no treasure. But he learned that a treasure ship loaded mostly with silver had recently left for Panama. Just north of the equator *The Golden Hind* overtook her. Although the galleon was unarmed the ship's master gave token argument. Drake quickly convinced him that no resistance was possible by firing a salvo from his cannons, then capturing the prize. This enormous cargo of gold, silver bars and silver coins, estimated to be worth 360,000 pesos, a huge fortune, was taken on board *The Golden Hind*. There was no violence. The Spanish captain and crew were released with their ship within a few days. They were left with a warning message to the Viceroy of Peru not to harm four Englishmen in his prison or else Drake would kill 2,000 Spaniards.

Now the object was to get home. The galleon had been taken on March 1, 1579. By mid-March Drake reached Costa Rica, where he found a ship with two pilots experienced in sailing to the Philippines. He took them aboard his ship with their charts.

Drake sailed north to Mexico, where another small ship of only slight value was taken. At the Mexican port of Guatulco he pillaged the city and took on considerable water estimated to be enough for a three month voyage. Here the two pilots taken in Nicaragua, and the pilot captured in the Cape Verde Islands, were released. Then Drake headed north, hoping to find the Strait of Anian and an easy way back to England.

From Guatulco he sailed due west, went far out to sea, then sailed northeast to hit the coast where the Northwest Passage was said to be. A navigation error led him far south, to landfall at the southern Oregon coast. He looked for a harbor to repair a leak.

Coming south along that rocky coast, somewhere just north of San Francisco, Drake found what he was looking for. The precise site has been argued about for decades. Scholars now agree that he stopped in what we call Drake's Bay. Almost certainly Drake didn't enter San Francisco Bay as accounts of the voyage would have noted that vast harbor. He must have satisfied himself that no Northwest Passage existed.

Drake stayed in California from June 17 to July 23, 1579. He careened his ship and explored some of the surrounding countryside.

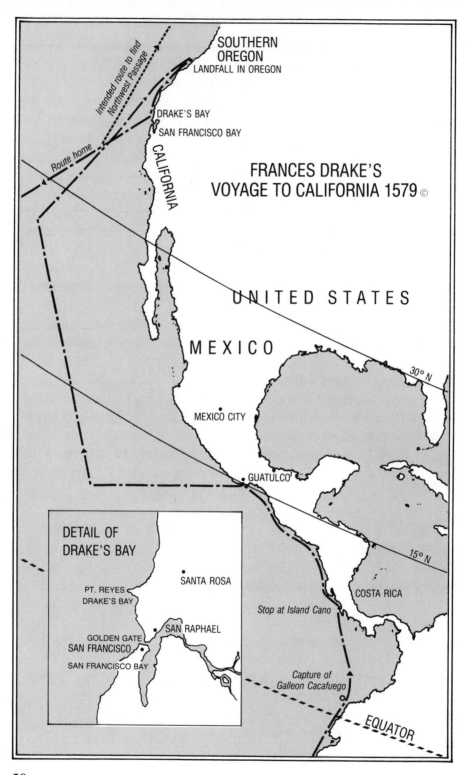

FRANCES DRAKE'S
VOYAGE TO CALIFORNIA 1579 ©

SOUTHERN
OREGON
LANDFALL IN OREGON

Intended route to find
Northwest Passage

Route home

DRAKE'S BAY

SAN FRANCISCO BAY

CALIFORNIA

UNITED STATES

MEXICO

30° N

MEXICO CITY

GUATULCO

15° N

DETAIL OF
DRAKE'S BAY

SANTA ROSA

PT. REYES
DRAKE'S BAY

COSTA RICA

Stop at Island Cano

SAN RAPHAEL

GOLDEN GATE
SAN FRANCISCO
SAN FRANCISCO BAY

Capture of
Galleon Cacafuego

EQUATOR

50

The Golden Hind is careened and repaired at Drake's Bay.
The ship was unloaded and beached to repair the hull.

Upon his arrival the local Indians came to visit. They were impressed, thinking Drake to be a god. A crown was placed on his head and long speeches were made by the Indian chief. Drake put a plate of brass on a stout post and claimed California as Nova Albion (New England) for his Queen. The weather was not to his liking. According to his chroniclers there were "stinking fogges" (fogs in summer certainly are usual) and snow on the nearby hills (harder to believe).

After repairing the ship and replenishing wood and water, Drake set sail west. The first landfall was in late September. He visited the Palau Islands at about 8 degrees north latitude and had a skirmish there with Polynesians. Then he sailed two weeks west to the Philippines and to present day Indonesia. On the island of Ternate six tons of cloves were taken on board. The ship was careened on an island near Indonesian Celebes.

On January 8, 1580 *The Golden Hind* ran aground off Celebes but got off the reef by lightening the ship. Three tons of cloves and two cannon were thrown overboard. Drake continued through the Indonesian Islands, arriving at Java, where he stayed for two weeks. Then he sailed around the Cape of Good Hope, with a stop at Sierra Leone in Africa to

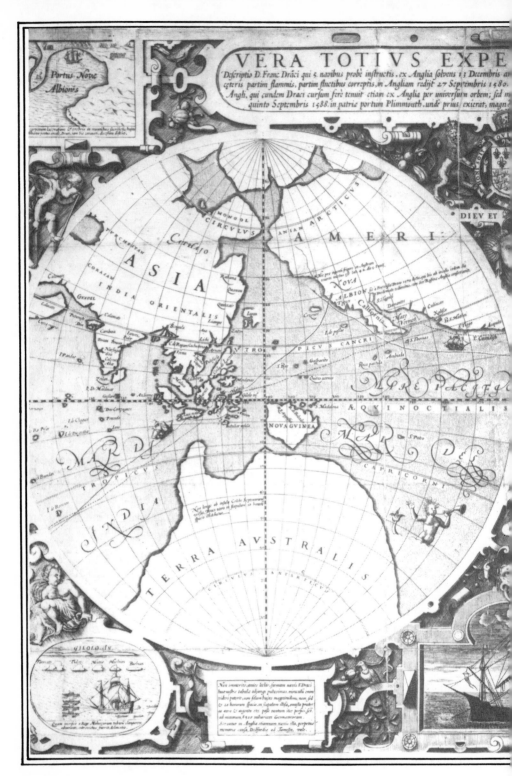

52 *An antique English map shows Drake's route in circumnavigating the globe.*

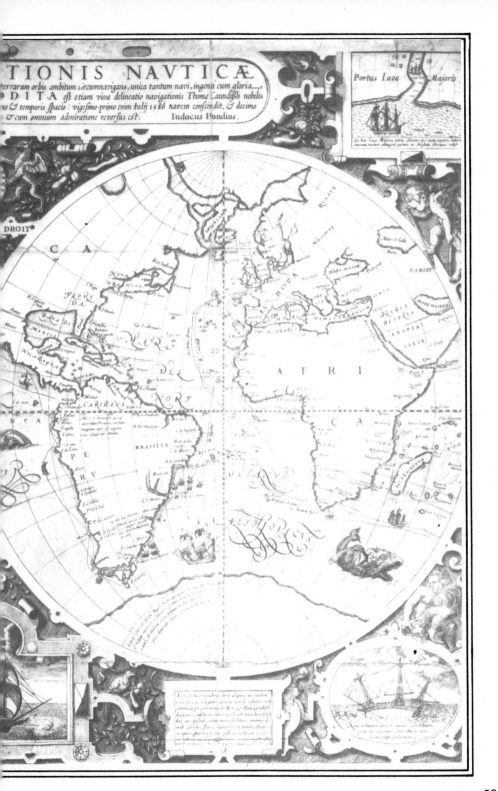

reprovision for the final trip home. On September 26, 1580 *The Golden Hind* landed at Plymouth.

Drake's return received a mixed reaction in England . His circumnavigation of the globe was the first by an Englishman and the booty was enormous. But news of the piracy had reached Europe a year earlier and the Spanish demanded the return of their treasure. Queen Elizabeth, fearing that Spain might go to war over Drake's activities, waited several days to see how strong the Spanish response would be. Soon, however, Drake was ordered to London for a private conversation with her. The Queen had decided that the Spanish would do nothing disastrous.

Drake was allowed to keep 10% of the treasure, the crew was given 10%, the crown and the financial backers got the rest. A token restoration was made to Spain. Elizabeth knighted Drake on his ship in 1581, thereby giving to him her official approval. Drake became a national hero, the first from the lower classes. Later he was Vice-Admiral of the forces that defended England against the Spanish armada in 1588.

Sir Francis Drake made other raiding voyages to Spain, Portugal and the Caribbean, but the loot from these adventures never equalled that of the captured Spanish galleon. He died at sea from dysentery in the Caribbean on January 18, 1596.

Because of inadequate resources England failed to follow up Drake's exploration of California. Also, Spain quickly armed her Pacific ships and later English pirates had scant success. California, a long way from England, continued to remain untouched by Europeans.

CHAPTER 6
THE GALLEONS FROM MANILA
1565-1815

GOLD AND SILVER WERE NOT THE ONLY TREASURES sought by Europeans in the newly seized lands of Asia and the Western Hemispere. Spices, given a value we would consider fantastic, were searched for in the East Indies. Various spices were used to preserve and flavor food, which was often at the point of spoiling. Of course, there was little or no refrigeration or other means of preservation except the use of salt.

Spain and Portugal both made claims to the East Indies because of the spices found there. Spain based its claim for the Philippines on their discovery in 1519 by Ferdinand Magellan's expedition. The Portuguese had acquired the Malucca Islands, to the south at the equator. In 1493 Pope Alexander IV tried to settle the dispute. He divided the world into two halves by running lines from the North and South Poles, through the Pacific and Atlantic Oceans. His interest, and felt authority, was to designate responsibility between Spain and Portugal for the conversion of the newly found "infidels" to Christianity.

In Asia the line was at 140 degrees east longitude. In the Atlantic the line ran 370 leagues (a league is about three miles) west of the Cape Verde Islands off Africa. Spain got the West Indies, Mexico, Central and South America except Brazil. In Asia Portugal received the Philippines and the Maluccas.

Portugal could reach its colonies in the Orient by sailing around the tip of Africa into the Indian Ocean. Spain agreed to sail to Asia only in the opposite direction, from Mexico. In 1529 an adjustment was made in the line. The King of Spain paid Portugal 350,000 ducats to gain possession of the Philippine Islands and both countries agreed to respect the other's territory. The Philippines were named in honor of Phillip II of Spain.

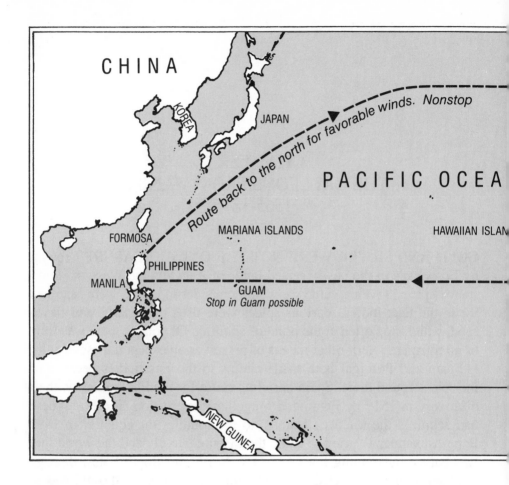

The islands were of doubtful value. There were clove trees in the Maluccas but only some cinnamon grew in the Philippines. Cinnamon, though scarce, wasn't valuable enough to justify the enormous trip across the Pacific to carry it to Europe. So Spain gave up its interest in spices, to think more about transshipping luxury goods from Asiatic countries to New Spain. Silver from Mexico would buy thousands of different things brought to Manila from China, Japan, India, and the islands of the Far East.

The practical difficulties of the voyages to and from Mexico were enormous. Sailing from the west coast of Mexico to Manila was feasible, as there was a following wind the entire distance and the voyage only took about three months. A stop at Guam on the way after 60-65 days could be made. Getting back to Acapulco was the problem.

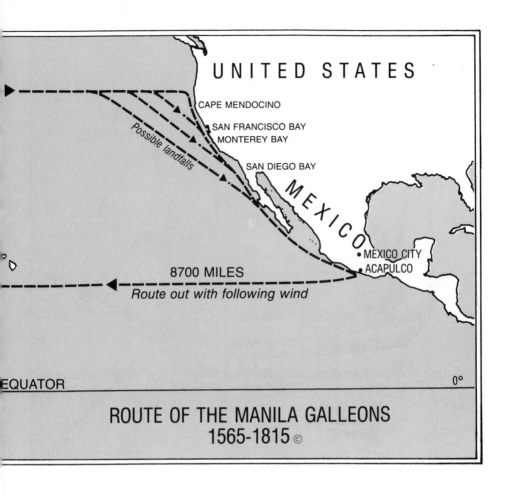

ROUTE OF THE MANILA GALLEONS
1565-1815 ©

In 1528 Alvarado de Saavedra sailed to the East Indies from Mexico but he couldn't find a way back against the prevailing winds and died in the Malaysian islands. A prize was then offered to the mariner who could find the winds to New Spain. In 1564 Andres de Urdaneta piloted an expedition that sailed far to the north and reached California at 37-39 degrees north latitude, somewhere north of San Francisco. Then the ships sailed down the California coast to Mexico.

The round trip of the Manila galleons to Acapulco, Mexico began in 1565. This dangerous voyage was made only once each year. The schedule continued for an amazing 250 years, until 1815, finally ending with the defeat of the Spanish monarchy in the Napoleonic wars.

Manila became an enclave of rich Spanish families living in a walled city, using Chinese for manual labor. Doing little to develop the islands,

A Spanish Galleon. These were slow, bulky ships with a high sterncastle.

the Spanish in the Philippines lived off the galleon trade. Even the clergy participated as traders, as church monies were used to finance commerce. In 1783 the Spanish population of Manila was less than 2,000 people. Financial power became concentrated in the hands of a few families. In 1586 there were 194 shippers. Two centuries later there were only 28 shippers.

A galleon was crewed with 150-250 men. The sailing of 1606 lost 80 men; the galleon of 1620 had 99 deaths. In 1657 a galleon was found drifting toward the tropics south of Acapulco with the entire crew dead.

It had left Manila over a year earlier. Despite these dangers there were many volunteers to sail on the ships. Profits of the trip were shared with the crew and survivors could count on being rich for the rest of their lives.

The crews' were made up mostly of adventurers. Ships officers were often political appointees. Sailing skills were slim. A few seasoned pilots were the only officers with nautical experience and the actual direction of the voyage was turned over to them. The pilots were from different nations, being Spanish, Portuguese, English, French, Irish. Crewmen were commonly Oriental.

The galleons themselves were made from teak and mahogany in the Orient. Most were built in the Philippines, some in Japan and Siam. They had a high forecastle and stern, offset by a broad beam. A typical ship was about 175 feet long with a 25 foot deep hold. Tonnage was usually 400 tons. Later in the 1700s some ships were as large as 1,000 or 1,700 tons.

A seagoing Chinese junk of the early 1800s.

At the height of the trading activity 20 to 50 large Oriental junks, with crews up to 300 men, came to Manila once a year for the bargaining. The most profitable cargo was silk, packed in precisely made crates. Resident Chinese in Manila skillfully loaded the ships. One galleon transported 50,000 pairs of women's silk stockings; another contained 80,000 women's combs. Other cargo included bolts of fine taffeta, damask, some cotton and a little tea and spices. Also carried were fans, carved ivory, diamond rings, gold, brass bells, jade, jasper, precious stones in jewelry, eye glasses, oriental screens, inlaid boxes, and other bric-a-brac.

Sailors often packed their sea chests with personal purchases they hoped to sell privately. Space for provisions necessary for the voyage was sometimes used for cargo and the ships were often overloaded. Cheating at all levels was prevalent. When the ship reached Acapulco the cargo was auctioned off at a fair. Most buyers were the aristocracy of New Spain. Some of the items were sent to Europe for resale.

Despite the huge profits, the logistics were distressing to the Spanish crown. The Japanese government refused to let Spanish ships stop and reprovision. The Spanish were unwanted in Japan, as Christian and European influences were considered incompatible with Japanese culture. Any visiting Spanish ship was confiscated.

In Spain merchants complained about the competition to their domestic cloth and wares, caused by importing Oriental goods. The King tried to placate them by restricting traffic to one galleon a year.

Interception of the galleons by pirates was never a major problem. The vast Pacific Ocean was so far from Europe that pirates looked to other seas for prizes. The galleons were armed, and carried about 80 cannons, but they rarely needed to fight. In 1587, however, Thomas Cavendish of England did take a galleon and three others were seized by Englishmen during the 1700's.

Dangers to a galleon's crew on the voyage east were terrible. The trip lasted about six months without touching land. Besides storms, disease was devastating. Food consisted mostly of biscuits, salted meat, salted fish, beans, bacon, cheese, vegetable oil, vinegar, onions, garlic, and other vegetables. Only sharks and dogfish could sometimes be caught. Vitamin deficiency diseases were present in the entire crew with often fatal results. Scurvy (vitamin C deficiency), beriberi (vitamin b1 deficieny), and pellagra (nicotinic acid deficiency) took a great toll of life.

The problems of disease and reprovisioning were never resolved. Stories existed about two islands—Rico de Oro (Rich in Gold) and Rico de Plata (Rich in Silver)—located somewhere on the way to New Spain, off the coast of Japan. Although the Spanish looked for them as their best hope, the islands were mythical. Supposedly the occupation of Alta California was delayed 150 years because of the continued belief in Rico de Oro and Rico de Plata (The Hawaiian Islands, discovered in 1778 by the Englishman, Captain James Cook, were never discovered by the Spanish). As a second choice in the search for a provisioning stop, the crown decided to further explore the foggy, dangerous, unsettled coast of Alta California.

CHAPTER 7
THE VOYAGES OF SEBASTIAN R. CERMENO 1595-6
AND
SEBASTIAN VISCAINO 1602-3

ONCE THE MANILA GALLEON established a regular run to Mexico, finding a haven in Alta California became an important consideration. The Spanish crown also worried about other European nations infringing on the area. Drake had claimed Nova Albion for England and there was the still unsettled possibility of a northwest passage, which would give easy access to California from the Atlantic Ocean.

In 1595, some 16 years after Drake visited California, Viceroy Luis de Valesco sponsored another voyage to explore the area. Sebastian Cermeno, a Portugese pilot, was chosen for the job. His ship, the *San Agustin*, capacity 200 tons, was a galleon. Cermeno agreed to the task if he could take on some silver for whatever trade might be possible. The ship contained 130 tons of cargo to help pay expenses. A prefabricated launch in three parts was also carried on board.

The *San Agustin* left Manila on July 5, 1595 and reached California near Crescent City in November but storms and the rocky shore made a landing impossible. The ship then sailed south to the point now called Drake's Bay, just north of San Francisco. The *San Agustin* anchored about 400 yards off shore and the launch was assembled, to explore the area. A month later a sudden storm drove the ship ashore and it broke up. A dozen sailors drowned and the entire cargo, including all the ship's provisions, was lost. Numerous ship spikes, nails and pieces of Chinese porcelain have been uncovered in nearby Indian burial mounds. Archeologists believe these came from the San Agustin and from dishes given to the Indians by Francis Drake.

Some 80 men crowded into the launch, to continue their voyage to Mexico. Cermeno tried to explore the California coast but the crowded

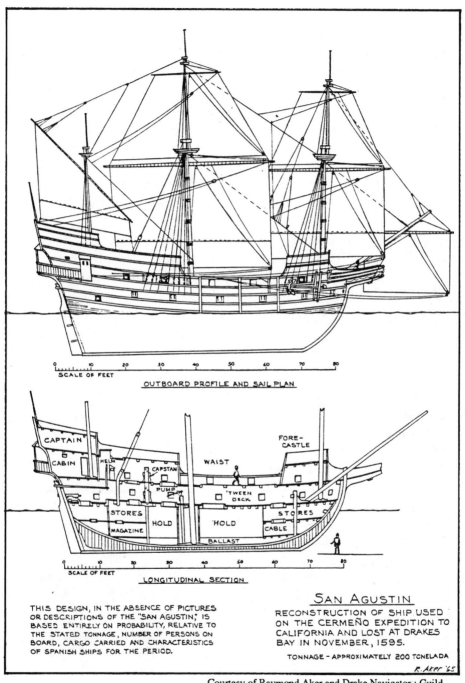

SCALE OF FEET

OUTBOARD PROFILE AND SAIL PLAN

CAPTAIN

CABIN HELM

CAPSTAN

PUMP

STORES

MAGAZINE

HOLD

WAIST

FORE-
CASTLE

'TWEEN
DECK

STORES

CABLE

HOLD

BALLAST

SCALE OF FEET

LONGITUDINAL SECTION

THIS DESIGN, IN THE ABSENCE OF PICTURES
OR DESCRIPTIONS OF THE "SAN AGUSTIN," IS
BASED ENTIRELY ON PROBABILITY, RELATIVE TO
THE STATED TONNAGE, NUMBER OF PERSONS ON
BOARD, CARGO CARRIED AND CHARACTERISTICS
OF SPANISH SHIPS FOR THE PERIOD.

SAN AGUSTIN

RECONSTRUCTION OF SHIP USED
ON THE CERMEÑO EXPEDITION TO
CALIFORNIA AND LOST AT DRAKES
BAY IN NOVEMBER, 1595.

TONNAGE – APPROXIMATELY 200 TONELADA

R. Aker '65

Courtesy of Raymond Aker and Drake Navigator's Guild.

63

boat made exploration difficult. They missed San Francisco Bay but saw the Farallon Islands. Monterey Bay, Morro Bay, and the islands near Santa Barbara were visited but in the process the men almost starved. At Santa Catalina Island they were saved when a huge wounded fish was discovered between some rocks. The fish, probably a large tuna, was large enough for the men to feast upon for eight days. The exhausted and distressed crew decided to sail as directly as possible to Mexico, and they brought the launch into Acapulco on January 31, 1596. Everyone survived.

Some knowledge was gained by this voyage but a board of inquiry was held to fix responsibility for the loss of the *San Agustin*. The officers blamed each other for the disaster. No definite fault could be found. A later report blamed the captain more than the weather for the shipwreck.

The last of the early explorers, though more a merchant than a sailor, was Sebastian Viscaino. He contracted with the Viceroy to explore the coasts of Baja and Alta California for pearls and a safe harbor for the Manila galleons. Three ships were fitted out for this voyage. In 1602 they coasted along t!.e entire California coast as far north as Cape Mendocino. Point Reyes, Drake's Bay, Monterey Bay, and Morro Bay were

China pottery chards found in the Drake's Bay area. On the left the edges are sharp and the glazes are dated to the time Drake visited the area. This China is thought to be from pottery given by Drake to the local Indians and used by them for ornamentation. The piece on the right has smooth edges from surf tumbling, has a glaze dating from the wreck of the San Agustin period, and is believed to come from the wreck of that ship.

Courtesy of Lowie Museum of Anthropology, University of California, Berkeley.

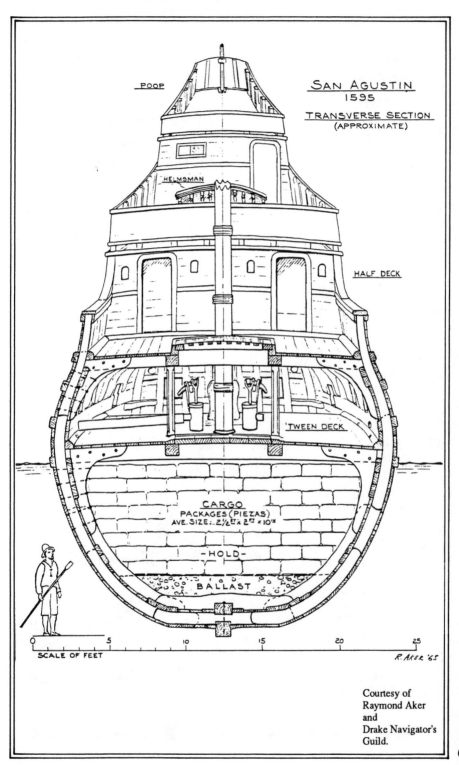

POOP

SAN AGUSTIN
1595

TRANSVERSE SECTION
(APPROXIMATE)

HELMSMAN

HALF DECK

'TWEEN DECK

CARGO
PACKAGES (PIEZAS)
AVE. SIZE: 2½ᶠᵗ x 2ᶠᵗ x 10ᴵⁿ

—HOLD—

BALLAST

0   5   10   15   20   25

SCALE OF FEET

R. AKER '65

Courtesy of
Raymond Aker
and
Drake Navigator's
Guild.

THE VOYAGES OF SEBASTIAN CERMENO AND SEBASTIAN VISCAINO ©

OREGON

Voyage of Viscaino from Acapulco

COQUILLE RIVER

Landfall of Cermeno's ship from Manila

CAPE BLANCO

PT. ST. GEORGE

CAPE MENDOCINO

Wreck of Cermeno's San Agustin

DRAKE'S BAY

SAN FRANCISCO BAY

Continuation of Cermeno's voyage in his launch

CALIFORNIA

SANTA CATALINA ISLAND

SAN DIEGO BAY

PACIFIC OCEAN

MEXICO

CHACALA ● ● COMPOSTELLA

Most of San Agustin survivors debarked at Chacala. Launch was then taken to Acapulco.

ACAPULCO

KEY
CERMENO'S ROUTE, 1595-1596 **- - - - -**
VISCAINO'S ROUTE, 1602-1603 **━ ━**

66

visited. They finally turned back because of illness in the crew. Viscaino gave an enthusiastic report in favor of establishing a settlement at Monterey for the galleons. The Viceroy seemed favorably disposed. A newly appointed Viceroy, however, didn't think a settlement in Monterey worth the trouble, as any galleon could reach Acapulco after sailing only a few more weeks. And no large quantities of pearls had been found. The Viceroy took comfort in the fact that no Northwest Passage had been discovered. Viscaino reaped little praise or money for his efforts.

Monterey never became a regular port of call for the Manila galleons. Unfavorable winds, fears of shipwreck and loss of cargo made captains very cautious about stopping there.

CHAPTER 8
ESTABLISHING THE MISSIONS
OF ALTA CALIFORNIA
Father Junipero Serra

VISCAINO'S RECOMMENDATION IN 1602 that Monterey Bay would make an ideal reprovisioning port found little favor with the Spanish bureaucracy. Hope persisted that the legendary Islands of Silver and Gold would be discovered in the north Pacific. The Manila galleons continued their annual trading voyages, with great loss of crews.

By the 1660's Spain had begun to weaken as a European power. The gold and silver brought from the New World produced inflation at home and Spain could not keep up with European rivals in commerce and manufacturing. Its possessions in New Spain were held by force of arms, but there was less money available for the army and navy.

Alta California had no obvious usefulness. The climate was good, but no treasure had been found there. Exploration was difficult and dangerous for ships. Grizzly bears were a real hazard to men and their beasts. The local Indians, sullen and unreliable, produced little of value for Europeans.

Even so, Spain wanted to hold on to Alta California. In the 1700's the Russians had come farther and farther south from Alaska, hunting sea otters for their downy fur. The old fear, that the English might find an easy northwest passage from the Atlantic and lay claim to the area, still existed (Amazing as it might seem to us, the non-existence of the Strait of Anian wasn't finally proven until the 1820's). A greater Spanish presence was needed in Alta California. Establishing a base for the Manila galleon at Monterey Bay would be a beginning.

In 1766 King Carlos III decided that new land and sea expeditions would be sent to explore California. Three major planners were involved: the King's agent, Visitor General Jose de Galvez; the area civil

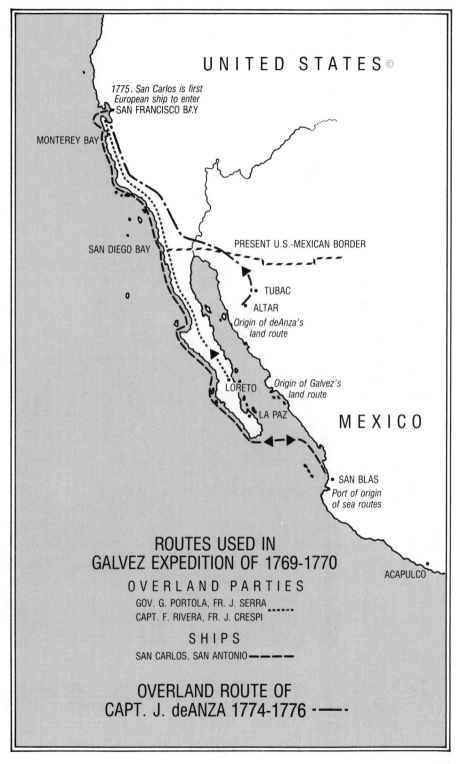

UNITED STATES©

1775, San Carlos is first
European ship to enter
SAN FRANCISCO BAY

MONTEREY BAY

SAN DIEGO BAY

PRESENT U.S.-MEXICAN BORDER

• TUBAC

ALTAR
Origin of deAnza's
land route

LORETO

Origin of Galvez's
land route

LA PAZ

MEXICO

• SAN BLAS
Port of origin
of sea routes

ROUTES USED IN
GALVEZ EXPEDITION OF 1769-1770

OVERLAND PARTIES

GOV. G. PORTOLA, FR. J. SERRA
CAPT. F. RIVERA, FR. J. CRESPI

SHIPS

SAN CARLOS, SAN ANTONIO

OVERLAND ROUTE OF
CAPT. J. deANZA 1774-1776

ACAPULCO

and military commander, Caspar de Portola, who would coordinate the governmental and military aspects; and the Franciscan priest, Junipero Serra, Father-President of the College of San Fernando in Mexico City, who would establish missions. The effort became known as the Galvez Expedition.

Father Junipero Serra. The only known authentic portrait.

The hope was that by creating a coordinated civil, military, and religious establishment, Alta California could be made a permanent and secure Spanish colony. Missions would convert and civilize the Indians. Presidios (forts) would be their protectors. Eventually pueblos (towns)

The mission at Carmel in partial ruin.

would evolve, where the Indians could live outside the missions. As a start, settlements were to be made at Monterey and San Diego.

About 225 men with different skills were recruited and divided into four divisions. Two went by sea, two went overland to San Diego Bay and then proceeded to Monterey Bay.

The two ships, the *San Carlos* and the *San Antonio*, both brigantines, were less than 80 feet long and carried a division each. The *San Carlos* sailed from San Blas, Mexico on January 10, 1769; the *San Antonio* left a month later. Both ships arrived in San Diego Bay in April, after great difficulty from head winds that blew them south. The *San Carlos* lost 24 of her crew from scurvy during the 110 day voyage. When the *San Antonio* arrived she received no welcome. The crew of the *San Carlos* was too weak to greet them.

The land divisions with cattle, horses, and mules arrived in May and June. Father Serra accompanied the first land division, which was commanded by Governor Portola; the second, with Captain Fernando Rivera as commander, had Father Juan Crespi to serve as its spiritual leader.

The *San Antonio* was sent back to San Blas with the sick. A relief ship from Mexico was lost at sea. After establishing a mission at San Diego Bay, the land parties proceeded north to look for Monterey Bay.

The march followed the coast past San Clemente and Santa Catalina Islands, past the future site of Los Angeles, then inland through the San Fernando Valley. Returning to the coast, it then went past Point Conception. The men continued on to Monterey Bay but failed to recognize it from Viscaino's grandiose description made over 160 years earlier. They marched further north and on November 2, 1769, a party of soldiers hunting deer were the first Europeans to see San Francisco Bay. The Spanish explorers did not realize they were seeing a huge, undiscovered harbor from their position on a ridge near San Bruno. The

The pueblo at San Jose.

Golden Gate was seen first not from the sea, but when the explorers trekked to the East Bay. It was not until 1775 that the first European ship, the *San Carlos*, entered San Francisco Bay.

The expedition returned south, again to Monterey Bay, but still didn't recognize it. A great cross was erected there. San Diego Bay was reached on January 13, 1770. The men were near starvation, about to give up and return to Mexico, when the San Antonio made port with new supplies.

A new expedition was organized to search for Monterey Bay and the *San Antonio* was dispatched to aid the men. Led by Governor Portola, the party marched north and reached Monterey Bay on May 24, 1770.

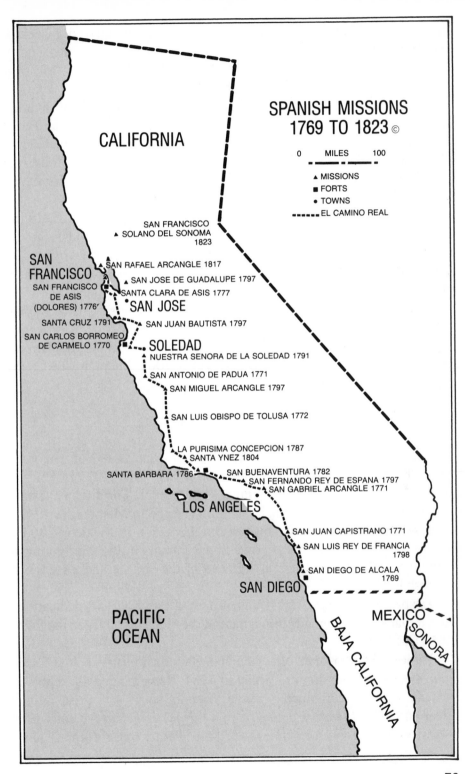

SPANISH MISSIONS
1769 TO 1823 ©

0   MILES   100

▲ MISSIONS
■ FORTS
● TOWNS
------- EL CAMINO REAL

CALIFORNIA

SAN FRANCISCO
▲ SOLANO DEL SONOMA
1823

SAN
FRANCISCO
SAN FRANCISCO
DE ASIS
(DOLORES) 1776

▲ SAN RAFAEL ARCANGLE 1817

▲ SAN JOSE DE GUADALUPE 1797

SANTA CLARA DE ASIS 1777

● SAN JOSE

SANTA CRUZ 1791

SAN CARLOS BORROMEO
DE CARMELO 1770

▲ SAN JUAN BAUTISTA 1797

SOLEDAD
▲ NUESTRA SENORA DE LA SOLEDAD 1791

▲ SAN ANTONIO DE PADUA 1771

▲ SAN MIGUEL ARCANGLE 1797

▲ SAN LUIS OBISPO DE TOLUSA 1772

▲ LA PURISIMA CONCEPCION 1787
▲ SANTA YNEZ 1804

SANTA BARBARA 1786 ▲ SAN BUENAVENTURA 1782
▲ SAN FERNANDO REY DE ESPANA 1797
▲ SAN GABRIEL ARCANGLE 1771

LOS ANGELES

▲ SAN JUAN CAPISTRANO 1771
▲ SAN LUIS REY DE FRANCIA
1798

▲ SAN DIEGO DE ALCALA
1769

SAN DIEGO

PACIFIC
OCEAN

MEXICO

BAJA CALIFORNIA

SONORA

This time the Bay was recognized. The *San Antonio* arrived a week later. Governor Portola presided at an official ceremony to dedicate the new colony. Father Serra conducted a mass, and on June 3, 1770, consecrated the Mission San Carlos Borromeo .

King Carlos III appropriated money to search for a new overland route from Sonora, Mexico to Monterey. In 1774 Captain Juan Batista de Anza, leading a company of 34 men, found a way along the Gila and Colorado Rivers, then turned westward to Monterey. In 1776 de Anza reached San Francisco Bay with 235 men and picked the site for a presidio and mission. He is considered the founder of San Francisco.

Between 1769 and 1823, 21 missions were founded in California. Placed about a day's journey apart (approximately 40 miles), the missions on El Camino Real (the King's Highway) stretched from San Diego to Sonoma. By 1824 the total mission population was about 21,000 Indians.

Presidios were erected in San Francisco, Monterey, Santa Barbara, and San Diego. Pueblos evolved in San Jose (1777), Los Angeles (1781), and Santa Cruz (1791). The pueblos had a total population of about 100 families. In 1800 there were only 200 soldiers in Alta California, with an additional 90 volunteers.

Father Junipero Serra

Serra was born in 1713 on the Mediterranean island of Majorca, a part of Spain. He became a Franciscan monk when only sixteen years old, afterwards a priest and church intellectual. For fifteen years he taught philosophy at a Roman Catholic college in Majorca. In 1749 he was sent to teach at the College of San Fernando in Mexico City. Half of his time was spent ministering to the Indians in the villages outside the city. Father Serra became the head of the college and a recognized church leader.

Despite sometimes frail health, his religious zeal and dedication to the Indians' welfare made him a natural candidate to advance the faith in Alta California.

Father Serra, 56 years old when he began his ministry in Alta California, died at the mission in Carmel in 1784. Remembered as an able and saintly man, he combined a gentle, friendly spirit with great religious zeal and administrative genius. He is the acknowledged creator of the mission system and sometimes called the "Father of California." The revered priest is being considered for sainthood by Roman Catholic Church authorities. Many, however, oppose the canonization because of Spanish cruelty to the Indians during the mission days.

The missions have become bathed in a romantic air, with the Indians supposedly living a simple but religious life in their sunny California. Actually the mission system was never successful and lasted only a little more than 50 years. It was difficult to get desirable people to emigrate from established comforts in Mexico to the new frontier. Father Serra complained that most of the European colonists were criminals. Until an irrigation system could be built, it was hard to grow food in the dry summers. The farming tools were incredibly primitive, scarcely better than sticks.

The soldiers went unpaid for years. There was constant strife with the Indians over the behavior of the soldiers, who often raped the Indian women, causing syphilis to become widespread. Once the Indians voluntarily converted to Christianity, they weren't allowed to leave the missions. Fugitives were hunted down and whipped. The Spanish had little of material value to offer the Indians.

Supply ships often failed to come from Mexico with manufactured goods, yet the Spanish government was fearful of commerce with visiting French, English, Russian and American ships, although these orders were increasingly ignored.

Officials on ships from other nations couldn't help recognizing the impotence of the Spanish presidios. In 1786 two French frigates, on a world circling scientific tour and commanded by Jean Francis La Perouse, called at Monterey for ten days. The English explorer, Captain George Vancouver, visited three times. Vancouver was received cordially in 1792 but during his second visit in 1793, fearful that he would see how weak they were, the Spanish restricted his inspection as much as possible. Vancouver reported to his government on the obvious weakness of the Spanish settlements.

In the 1790's American ships, interested in trading finished goods for sea otter pelts, began arriving at Monterey. For a time they formed a partnership with the Russians. Goods from New England were traded for sea otter furs gathered by the Russians with their Alaskan Indian hunters. The mission cattle herds grew and the Americans began trading for hides, to make leather goods on the east coast of the United States.

Beginning in 1811, Spain was increasingly threatened by revolution in Mexico. Trade and money to the missions virtually stopped. Soldiers went unpaid. The missions were on their own, except for some illegal bartering with American and Russian ships. Monterey was sacked by the French-Argentinian pirate, Bouchard, who demanded surrender of the province! The weak Spanish forces temporarily withdrew to the interior and Bouchard soon vanished.

A growing Spanish population in California coveted the modest wealth of the mission lands. In 1813 the government in Mexico City provided for the division of the lands to nonreligious owners, mostly the Indians—the original goal when the missions had been established. In 1821 the Spanish government of New Spain was overthrown, and eventually the Mexican Republic was established. A Mexican plan was devised in 1834 to give half of the mission lands to the Indians, the rest to be held in trust, managed for religious purposes. 21 missions were converted to civil use during the next three years. The Indians soon squandered, or were swindled, out of their shares. Corrupt administrators put much land into private hands by making numerous fraudulent sales to cronies. In 1844 the remaining assets were sold to help finance the war between Mexico and the United States. The mission system had collapsed.

The missions fell into ruins. At San Raphael the building disappeared. Only the mission in Santa Barbara has been used without interruption for religious services. After 1900 various citizens groups, the Church, and the State of California rebuilt the missions we visit today.

CHAPTER 9
THE RUSSIANS IN CALIFORNIA AT FORT ROSS

THE RUSSIANS ESTABLISHED A PRESENCE at the northern edge of Alta California in the early 1800's.

Vitus Bering, a Dane employed by Russia, first explored Alaska, coming from Siberia. The Tsarist government wanted to exploit the huge numbers of otter furs found there. The Russian American Company began a settlement at Sitka, Alaska in 1799, with Alexander Baranoff as manager, and used Aleuts (Siberian natives) as hunters. The endeavor was extremely lucrative, because sea otters were greatly prized for their soft, luxuriant fur. Pelts were sold in China and Europe for as much as $150 each, an enormous price at the time.

Sitka got off to a bad start. In 1802 local Indians, the Tlingits, attacked the fort and killed most of the settlers. With a reinforced army of 1,000 men, Baranoff defeated the Tlingits two years later.

Keeping the town in food and manufactured goods was a desperate problem. A new agent appointed by the Tsar in 1805, Nikolai Rezanov, tried to remedy the situation, but only the visit of an American ship, the Juno, temporarily held off starvation.

The food situation in Sitka worsened. In 1806 Rezanov sailed to San Francisco on the *Juno*, to buy food and goods from the Spanish. A difficulty to overcome was the Spanish ban on all trade with foreign ships.

By the time the ship arrived at San Francisco, half the sailors were ill from scurvy and unable to work. The Russians used their distress to beg entry to the port. Rezanov was unsuccessful in his quest until he met Dona Conception Arguello, the 15 year old daughter of the Commandant. A romance developed between the girl and the middle-aged widower. He proposed marriage and she accepted. Food was purchased. Rezanov sailed back to Sitka, but died returning to Europe. The betrothed Dona Conception never married and devoted herself to good works, not

*Nikolai Rezanov, agent of
the Russian America Company,
which established Fort Ross.*

learning the fate of her prospective husband until 1842. She died in 1857. A famous California romance.

The Spanish never controlled the coast north of San Francisco. A settlement on Vancouver Island in Canada had been abandoned and a proposed site at Bodega never materialized.

The Russians and their Aleuts continued hunting the sea otter. In 1817 they established a fort at the site of Fort Ross, on a windy bluff about 60 miles north of San Francisco. The Aleuts took as many as 1,000 pelts a month. By 1828 the otters had been decimated, and hunters were only skinning 100 pelts a year

An attempt was made to farm the area, in the hope food could be grown to supply Sitka. But the thin topsoil, cool climate, and hilly terrain made farming difficult, and the attempt, overall, was a failure. In 1841 Fort Ross (Russ) was abandoned.

John Sutter, the Swiss empire builder in pre-Gold Rush days, purchased all of Russia's California possessions. Mostly he was interested in the hardware at Fort Ross. He wanted what the Russians left behind for use in his own fort at Sacramento. For 30,000 pesos he got all the land, from the coast to 12 miles inland and from Point Reyes to Cape Mendocino. But as no one had secure title, the land wasn't worth the cost, and Sutter soon lost it in the cataclysmic changes American sovereignty and the Gold Rush brought in 1848.

The Russians retreated to Alaska, leaving their names to a few places in Northern California. In 1867 the Russian government sold Alaska to the United States for 7.2 million dollars, about two cents an acre, and Russia left North America.

Fort Ross became a State Park in 1906. It has been restored after a series of disastrous fires. The surrounding area is used mainly for grazing cattle and sheep.

By 1916 the sea otters had been hunted almost to extinction. Protected now, they are making a comeback and are fairly common in Southern California. Left alone, they will again flourish near Fort Ross.

Courtesy Bancroft Library, University of California, Berkeley.

A French rendering of Fort Ross as it was in 1828.

CHAPTER 10
AMERICANS OVERTHROW MEXICAN RULE
Thomas O. Larkin, American Consul

A WEAK SPAIN, incapable of continued control of Mexico and California, was forced by revolutionaries to accept Mexican independence in 1821. Augustin de Iturbide, a Mexican army officer, established an empire in 1822 and crowned himself emperor, but he was soon overthrown. A republic was established the next year.

The new government was feeble and unstable. Alta and Baja California were provinces governed by feuding political factions and their supporting small armies. Newly appointed governors often came and quickly left Monterey, Alta California's capital.

The mission system was ending. In 1824 there were about 18,000 Indians in the missions, with only 4200 non-Indians. Indian rebellion was increasing. Attempts to get Mexicans to colonize California were unsuccessful. Many colonists came from Mexican jails.

The missions and private ranches had vast herds of cattle. Hides and tallow (made from animal fat) were the main exports, sold to Americans from New England. The hides were made into shoes and other leather goods on the East Coast; the tallow used for candles and soap. Hides were traded for everything from pianos to combs, as almost nothing was manufactured in California.

Life in California, though not luxurious, was simple and pleasant. Almost all work with cattle was done from horseback. Indians did most of the drudgery. The mild climate encouraged outdoor living. There were numerous church holidays, with feasts and fandangos. The military presence in the presidios consisted of a few soldiers, who were rarely paid, and a few ancient cannons. There were no cities of any consequence.

'Native Californians Lassoing a Steer' by A. Ferran

Americans began arriving in substantial numbers wanting to settle, but the Mexican government was wary of their intentions. New Englanders especially tended to be haughty and Puritanical. Many were frank in revealing their conviction that California was too good to be run by Mexicans. Yankee ingenuity, industry and morality, they felt, would do wonders for California. The Mexicans tried to integrate the Americans by offering them huge grants of land, with two conditions: that they become naturalized Mexican citizens and be baptized in the Roman Catholic Church. Most American settlers readily agreed to these terms, but kept their private convictions. A single land grant could be as large as 48,000 acres, or over 75 square miles. Combining the grants of family members might make a rancho over 300,000 acres.

In Washington, D. C. the concept of Manifest Destiny was on the rise. The American government felt an obligation to expand the country

BATTLES OF
BEAR FLAG REVOLT 1846
MEXICAN WAR IN CALIFORNIA
1846-1848©

from the Alantic to the Pacific Ocean. Relations between the United States and Mexico became difficult. On October 18, 1842, an American warship commanded by Thomas Jones, who thought the United States and Mexico were at war, sailed into Monterey Bay and seized the California capitol. Jones only realized his mistake after being convinced by the American representative in Monterey, Thomas Larkin. Commander Jones apologized, withdrew his troops, and sailed for Los Angeles, where he was honored by a dazzling ball at the home of Yankee businessman, Abel Stearns, and his Mexican bride.

In 1844 a company of American explorers led by Lieutenant John Frémont, with the famous scout, Kit Carson, arrived overland from Oregon. Their original assignment was to find safe land routes to the West Coast. Fremont wasn't welcomed by the Mexicans, who could do little but ask him to leave.

Texas gained its independence from Mexico in 1836 and was annexed to the United States in 1845. This precipitated the U. S.-Mexican War of 1846-1848. President Polk had tried to buy California for $40,000,000, but Mexico even refused to talk to his envoy. U. S. troops invaded Mexico, while Americans in California declared their independence in the Bear Flag Revolt. Although the battles were small, the consequences were immense.

Hostilities began when a band of twenty-four Americans, led by Ezekiel Merritt, believing that Mexico intended to force Americans to leave California, took over the town of Sonoma and arrested the military commander, General Mariano Vallejo. They then confiscated a herd of horses, before it was driven to Monterey for use by the Mexican army. On June 10, 1846, the Republic of California was established and William B. Ide, a rancher who had arrived in 1845, was elected President. William Todd, Mrs. Abraham Lincoln's nephew, made a flag from unbleached muslin and blackberry juice, with a single star, a drawing of a grizzly bear, and a lower border of green and red. General Vallejo was sent off to jail at Sutter's Fort. The Americans joined forces with regular U. S. troops when Commodore John Sloat sailed the U. S. warship, Portsmouth, into Monterey Bay on July 7th. Sloat met no opposition and seized the capitol in the name of the United States. The Republic of California ceased to exist on July 9th.

Although he had supposedly received secret orders from President Polk to encourage the Americans, Lt. John Fremont at first refused to join them in the rebellion. Finally he decided to combine forces and the

Courtesy Bancroft Library, University of California, Berkeley.

Drawing of Monterey in 1846 by Lt. J. W. Revere, U. S. Navy.
Revere was the grandson of Paul Revere, Revolutionary War hero.

the small army was called the California Battalion. Commodore Sloat turned his command over to Commodore Robert Stockton, who appointed Fremont military commander-in-chief in California and civilian governor. Forces were also joined with the naval troops.

San Diego and Los Angeles were occupied. Fremont left garrisons there and headed for northern California to recruit more troops. Pueblo Los Angeles soon revolted and ran the American soldiers out. San Diego was also retaken by Mexicans, but American troops led by Captain Zeke Meritt drove them out in a brisk sortie. Meanwhile, 300 reinforcements, commanded by General Stephen Kearny, were marching west through New Mexico.

A small battle was fought by a detachment of the California Battalion and Mexican lancers on the plains near the Salinas River. Four Americans and perhaps a dozen Californios (troops of the opposition) were killed. Kearny's Army of the West neared San Diego, where they were attacked by Mexican lancers led by Andres Pico. General Kearny was wounded, 20 of his men were killed, but the rest reached San Diego. Both sides claimed victory in the Battle of San Pascual. The Mexicans claimed only one of their soldiers was killed.

General Kearny recaptured Los Angeles in early 1847. The strength of the Mexican opposition was running out. Lt. Col. Fremont independently offered to accept the surrender of the Mexican forces. He had strengthed his position with the Californios several days earlier by reversing the death sentence of a Mexican leader, Totoi Pico, cousin of the lancers' commander. On January 13, 1847, Andres Pico surrendered the Mexican cause. The Mexican War, also called the Mexican War in California or the Conquest of California, was over.

California officially became U. S. property with the signing of the Treaty of Guadalupe Hidalgo on February 2, 1848 and became a state in 1850. Mexico was given $15,000,000 compensation for the loss of her territory west of Texas to the Pacific Ocean. Nine days before the treaty signing, on January 24, gold was discovered at Sutter's Mill.

Thomas O. Larkin, American Consul

There were no Washingtons or Jeffersons in the war for California independence. Many of the prominent Americans in that struggle had their faults, tending to bluster and act impetuously. In contrast, Thomas O. Larkin played a substantial and little appreciated role with his cool good sense and moderate temperament. Larkin was U. S. Consul to California from 1844 to 1848, with his office in Monterey. He was also the main source of information for the Washington government, as he'd been appointed a secret agent of Secretary of State Buchanan and President Polk in 1845. Slow communications reduced the importance of his advice.

Larkin was born in New England in 1802. Apparently his education was sketchy, as he was a terrible speller, although a prolific letter writer and record keeper. He came to California in 1832, employed by his half-brother, a sea captain trading with Hawaii and Alta California. In 1832 Larkin reached the village of Yerba Buena in San Francisco Bay. In 1833 he moved to Monterey and became a general merchant and hides and tallow trader.

Also in that year he married a young widow, whom he had met on the ship coming to California. She became the first American woman to live in California. Larkin built a two story house combining New England features with Spanish verandas and adobe walls. The house still exists as a State Monument. The couple raised six children; their first son, Thomas, was the first American child born in California.

*Thomas O. Larkin,
American Consul
to Mexican California.*

Courtesy Bancroft Library, University of California, Berkeley.

Thomas Larkin soon became the most influential American in Alta California. He was shrewd but tactful, financially successful, yet hospitable and generous. Mexicans liked him. Many times they asked him to accept their citizenship, but he always refused, not wishing to give up his American identity. It was inevitable that his government would ask him to represent its interests in California. Larkin acccepted the responsibility but continued his own business.

In 1846, upon the request of the U.S. government, Larkin wrote a 10,000 word report called "Description of California" and "Notes on Personal Character of the Principal Men." This described the missions, ships of call in 1845, listed and evaluated the prominent Mexicans and Americans. It was an inventory of California resources. He needed to hire, at his eventual personal expense, a good writer to copy out the reports and put them into finished form. Secretary Buchanan appreciated Larkin's effort but said that no precedent existed for paying a clerk to do this type of work!

In 1845 Larkin wrote to another early American arrival, the literate and usually enthusiastic John Marsh of San Jose. He told Marsh to "shake off your apathy and idleness" and write letters, describing California in a manner that would interest Americans to come West. Larkin said he would have them published in eastern newspapers.

Larkin tried to hold down the hot tempers of Americans who were bent on fighting the Mexicans in 1846. He believed that time and persuasion would bring Mexican California to the U. S., without war. He tried to convince Commodore Sloat not to run up the U. S. flag immediately after the American Navy entered Monterey Bay. Larkin wanted to wait two or three weeks in order to see if the Mexicans would voluntarily come over to the American side. His advice was ignored.

Once the war began, Larkin was taken prisoner by the Mexicans for a few months in late 1846 and early 1847. He was treated well, no doubt because of the high regard held for him by his captors.

In 1849 Larkin moved to San Francisco and increased his fortune by land speculation. Later he was a founder of the city of Benicia, and a participant in the gold rush. He was a member of the Constitutional Convention for California statehood held in 1849. Officially, California became a U.S. state in 1850. It came into the Union as a "free" or non-slavery state.

Thomas Larkin died in 1858 of typhoid fever. History gives him high marks, although he is only vaguely remembered for his efforts in the Mexican War in California.

James W. Marshall is standing in front of the small sawmill he constructed in partner-
ship with John Sutter on the American River at Colma. The date the daguerreotype
photograph was taken was January 19, 1848, five days before gold was discovered
here, starting the California Gold Rush.

PART II

THE AMERICAN ERA

John Charles Frémont as a Civil War General.

CHAPTER 11
John Charles Frémont, The Pathfinder

AS AMERICA BEGAN TO THINK OF ITSELF as a country capable of filling the continent between the Atlantic and Pacific Oceans, exact geographical information about the West was needed. Settlers began crossing the mountains to settle in English Oregon and Mexican California. Washington politicians sensed the beginning of an American migration to the Pacific. The 1802 expedition of Lewis and Clark for President Thomas Jefferson only began the western exploration.

On a four year cruise around the world, Lieutenant Charles Wilkes of the U.S. Navy had done detailed charting of the Oregon coast in 1841. He also sent a party of scientists and officers overland from Fort Vancouver in Oregon through the valleys of the Willamette and Sacramento Rivers, which was met by his ship in San Francisco.

President John Tyler gave the task of exploring and mapping the West to a 29 year old U. S. Army Lieutenant, John Charles Frémont, who had helped map the still wild regions of Minnesota, Iowa, and South Dakota. Frémont was married to the daughter of the powerful U.S. senator, Thomas Hart Benton, an advocate of western expansion.

Between 1842 and 1853 Frémont made five expeditions west, became a national hero because of his daring and public relations skills, but ended his life with a flawed reputation. His first expedition was made with 30 scouts and trappers. Senator Benton's 12 year old son, Randolph, went along as did Randolph's 19 year old cousin, Henry Brant. The government appropriated $30,000, with instructions to describe the topography, weather, Indians, plants and animals, hazards, and anything useful to future immigrants. The departure point was St. Louis. The men, with their horses, mules, ox carts, even a rubber boat, and daguerreotype camera, set off to explore the South Pass region through the Rocky Mountains, in present-day Wyoming.

The company followed the North Platte River, a route that later became the Oregon Trail, through the hunting grounds of the Arapahoes, Pawnees, Sioux, and Cheyennes, to the fur trapper's strongholds at St. Vrain's Fort on the South Platte and Fort Laramie on the North Platte. The legendary Kit Carson was their chief scout. The men travelled through the South Pass near present Caspar, Wyoming, then went north and west toward the Wind River Mountains. They had crossed the present state of Nebraska and most of Wyoming. Then they retraced their route back home. The trip took about four months, from mid-June to mid-October, 1842. Frémont's report of his observations found an enthusiastic, popular reception in the East.

The second expedition in 1843-44 was more ambitious than the first. Fremont crossed Kansas and eastern Colorado to St. Vrain's Fort, went through the South Pass and entered the Great Basin region, north of Great Salt Lake, between the Rockies and Sierra Nevadas. Then he followed the Snake and Columbia Rivers across Idaho and Oregon to Fort Vancouver, which was operated by the British Hudson Bay Company.

Fort Vancouver, on the Columbia River across from present Portland, Oregon, was the center of what civilization there was in the northwest. It had 22 major buildings to sustain the fur trappers. Frémont's party was received cordially. They refreshed themselves and replenished their supplies.

The party then headed south across Oregon and down the eastern slope of the Sierra Nevada Mountains, past Pyramid Lake in Nevada. It was the middle of winter, snow was deep, and the party was uncertain of its location. The men and animals were being worn down by the cold, snow, and near starvation. Horses, mules, even their dogs, were killed for food. The stress caused one man to temporarily become mentally ill. The local Indians used as guides had warned that their plan to cross the mountains in February was foolhardy. Eventually the Indians deserted.

Using snow shoes and the horses to break a trail through the snow, the men finally reached the summit of the Sierra Nevadas, and on St. Valentine's Day, 1844, became the first white men to see Lake Tahoe. On February 21st the Sacramento Valley could be seen to the west, and beyond, San Francisco Bay. On March 6th the company finally straggled out of the snow to safety at Sutter's Fort (present day Sacramento).

John Sutter himself welcomed the exhausted, ragged band and told Frémont about his dream of a private kingdom in California. The fort had been established five years earlier and was surpassed on the West

"Moving Camp" illustrates an account of a Frémont expedition.

Coast only by Fort Vancouver. The enclosure was approximately 320 by 160 feet, with shops of all kinds to carry on the work of the miniature empire. Indians did all the unskilled labor. Sutter had become a Mexican citizen but saw no reason not to be hospitable to the Americans. A number of American and European immigrants were already staying there.

Fremont's group remained 16 days, resupplied themselves, then headed south. They had lost or eaten about half of their animals. On leaving they were better off, with 130 horses and mules and 30 head of cattle.

For a few days a young Indian man guided Frémont through the San Joaquin Valley. Then the party entered the mostly uninhabited San Fernando Valley. Mexican authorities had been alerted to their presence and went to Sutter's Fort to investigate, but made no attempt to follow the explorer.

Across the Mohave Desert the Old Spanish Trail was found with the help of an Indian vaquero. Frémont crossed the desert, went through southern Nevada, crossed Utah, explored the headwaters of the Colorado and Arkansas Rivers, then recrossed the Rockies near Pueblo, Colorado. The men stopped at Bent's Fort in Colorado for an extended rest, before ending the journey at St. Louis. Frémont's report of the second expedition became a best seller, making the West live.

About 60 men, 150 horses, 250 cattle, and several Delaware Indians to hunt for food, went on Frémont's third expedition. Kit Carson again served as a scout. The objectives were vague. The approaching war between Mexico and the U.S. made California a logical prize and that region needed further examination. The expedition brought Captain Frémont to the position of military commander-in-chief of the American forces in California and eventually California's first governor. His part in the conquest of California also led to charges of insubordination and a court-martial.

The exploring party went by way of Bent's Fort, across the Rockies to Great Salt Lake, then followed the Humboldt River across Nevada to the eastern slope of the Sierra Nevadas. There the forces divided. Frémont and Kit Carson in one group looked for a pass through the mountains near Lake Tahoe. The other and larger group proceeded south under the direction of Theodore Talbot. Led by the scout, Old Joe Walker, it charted the pass through the Sierras now known as Walker Pass.

Captain Frémont made a relatively easy passage through present Donner Pass (named for the Donner Party, who were trapped there a year later). Snow had not yet begun to fall, although it was December. The party stayed at Sutter's Fort for a few days, then proceeded south, eventually rejoining the other group, south of present-day San Jose.

The Mexicans were most unhappy with Frémont's reappearance in their country. General Jose Castro informed Frémont by letter that the American was to leave immediately. Outmanned and outgunned, Captain Frémont assumed an insulted pose, but managed to avoid fighting with the Mexican forces. Meanwhile, unknown to people in faraway California, the Mexican War had started.

Initially, Frémont declined to lead Americans who wanted to take up arms, saying that his duties in California were not military. He explored the Sacramento Valley up to Oregon, engaging in fierce encounters with the Klamath Indians, both going north and returning south. Kit Carson led one attack that killed 175 Indians at the northern end of the valley. The Indians retaliated by killing three of Frémont's men. Another attack by Frémont killed 20 Indians.

Upon returning to the lower Sacramento Valley, Frémont learned that

Frémont's California Battalion enters Monterey in 1846.

war with Mexico had begun. Fearing the Indians would side with Mexico, Frémont's men slaughtered more natives.

The soldier decided to join the Bear Flaggers against the Mexicans. The California Battalion, led by Frémont, was established, consisting of Frémont's men and the American volunteers. Soon Frémont was appointed military commander-in-chief as well as civil governor by Commodore Robert Stockton. Frémont's forces captured San Diego and Los Angeles. Both cities were later lost to the Mexicans but recaptured by infantry reinforcements led by General Stephen Kearny.

Lieutenant Colonel Frémont independently arranged the surrender of the Mexicans. Feeling upstaged, General Kearny informed the upstart, junior officer that Frémont had no authority to be military commander and governor of California and demanded that Frémont surrender these positions. Frémont refused, saying his appointment was legitimate. He had seen the end of the Mexican War in California, although the final treaty wasn't signed until February, 1848.

Kearny and Frémont returned to the East with their troops overland. At Fort Leavenworth, Kansas, General Kearney had Frémont arrested for insubordination. A subsequent military court martial found Frémont guilty, but recommended leniency because of his past service, and the confusion of authority between General Kearny and Commodore Stockton. The President agreed with the court's finding but released Frémont from arrest and returned him to duty.

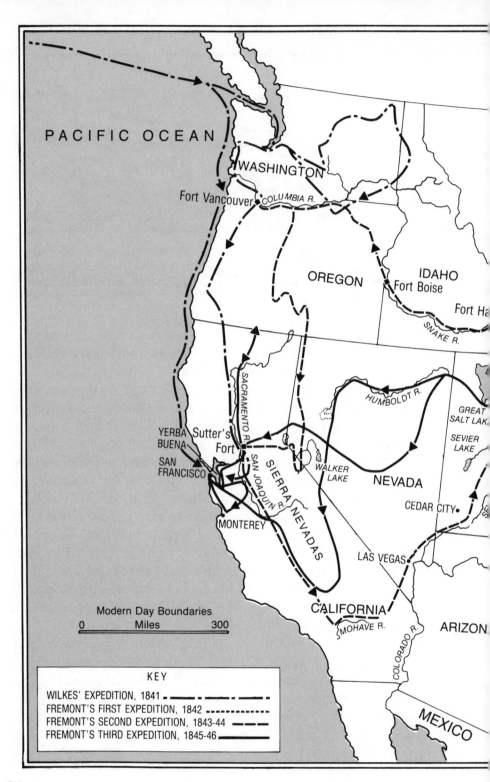

PACIFIC OCEAN

WASHINGTON

Fort Vancouver COLUMBIA R.

OREGON

IDAHO
Fort Boise

Fort Ha

SNAKE R.

HUMBOLDT R.

GREAT
SALT LAK

SEVIER
LAKE

SACRAMENTO R.

YERBA Sutter's
BUENA Fort

SAN
FRANCISCO

SAN JOAQUIN R.

SIERRA NEVADAS

WALKER
LAKE

NEVADA

CEDAR CITY •

MONTEREY

LAS VEGAS

CALIFORNIA

MOHAVE R.

COLORADO R.

ARIZON

MEXICO

Modern Day Boundaries
0   Miles   300

KEY

WILKES' EXPEDITION, 1841 ▪—▪—▪—▪
FREMONT'S FIRST EXPEDITION, 1842 ·············
FREMONT'S SECOND EXPEDITION, 1843-44 — — —
FREMONT'S THIRD EXPEDITION, 1845-46 ▬▬▬▬▬

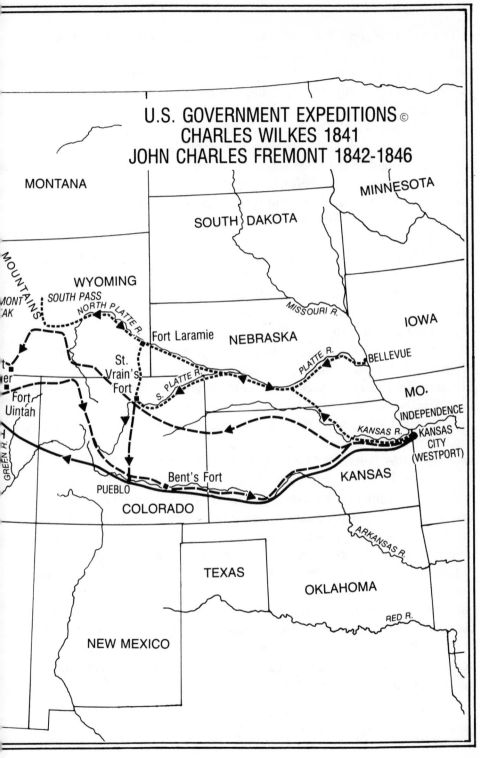

U.S. GOVERNMENT EXPEDITIONS ©
CHARLES WILKES 1841
JOHN CHARLES FREMONT 1842-1846

MONTANA

MINNESOTA

SOUTH DAKOTA

MOUNTAINS

WYOMING
SOUTH PASS

NORTH PLATTE R.

MONTAINS
AK

Fort Laramie

NEBRASKA

MISSOURI R.

IOWA

St.
Vrain's
Fort

S. PLATTE R.

PLATTE R.

BELLEVUE

Fort
Uintah

S. PLATTE R.

MO.

INDEPENDENCE

GREEN R.

KANSAS R.

KANSAS
CITY
(WESTPORT)

Bent's Fort

KANSAS

PUEBLO

COLORADO

ARKANSAS R.

TEXAS

OKLAHOMA

RED R.

NEW MEXICO

The explorer found himself free but with a tarnished reputation. There were no prospects for another government survey but Frémont's father-in-law found private backing for an expedition to determine the best route to California for the coming transcontinental railroad.

Thirty men signed on with Frémont and the party left Bent's Fort in mid-November, 1848. Despite much advice, they attempted to cross the San Juan Mountains of the Rockies in the middle of the worst winter in memory. Caught in the deep snow, they were in danger of either freezing or starving to death, before being rescued by help from Taos, New Mexico. Ten men died. Frémont ultimately led the survivors along the old Gila Trail across Arizona to Los Angeles.

A fifth expedition, also private, sought another good railroad route. Frémont found the Cochetopa Pass in the Rocky Mountains at 9000 feet elevation, where the buffalo were able to cross all year. This group of men also suffered hunger and cold weather but only one man froze to death. The Sierra Nevadas were crossed at Walker Pass.

Frémont and his wife bought land near Yosemite Valley and enjoyed a period of prosperity, particularly when gold was discovered on their property. For a year Frémont served as one of California's first U. S. Senators. In 1856 he became the Republican Party's first nominee for President, but lost to James Buchanan.

During the Civil War Frémont commanded the Army of the West, headquartered in St. Louis, but angered President Lincoln by issuing the war's first proclamation freeing the slaves in Missouri. Trying to hold the Union together, Lincoln feared this was premature and would anger Missouri residents, almost equally divided on the slavery issue. Frémont was reassigned, but resigned his army commission when placed under the command of a younger general. During 1878-1883 he served as Governor of the Arizona Territory. Frémont died in New York in 1890.

Like many heroes, Frémont seems a captive of early fame and adulation, a man unable to live up to his past exploits. A remarkably capable explorer and describer of our uncharted West-the man of action-his decisiveness struck many as arrogance and at times his daring was close to being foolhardy. And like many people of his time, Frémont could condone terrible acts of savagery against Indians, without justification. But he was a giant figure in California history.

CHAPTER 12
TO CALIFORNIA BY SHIP DURING THE GOLD RUSH

ON JANUARY 24, 1848, JAMES MARSHALL, a carpenter working with John Sutter on the construction of a sawmill on the American River, noticed golden flecks in the mill race. Within a few days tests proved that the flecks were really gold. The news filtered back East and eventually President Polk confirmed the discovery in an official announcement.

At the time Sutter's Fort had about 290 white settlers. San Francisco had a population of perhaps 350 people. Los Angeles was smaller.

Finding gold in California had a profound effect on East Coast population centers. Young men hoped to go to California, find gold, and return home rich. They also wanted to escape the confines of a staid society, and leave behind low wages with limited opportunities. The enthusiasm generated for a trip to California was enormous.

Young men were the Argonauts. They found plenty of encouragement from their elders, who provided the money. This was all done sensibly and properly. Most of the travelers organized into companies having 6 to 150 members. Agreements were signed to share alike the profits from mining and selling the goods they took with them to California. Gambling, swearing, and drinking were forbidden. Almost no women signed up.

How to go? There were two basic choices, overland or by sea. The hopeful adventurers took the way they were most comfortable with. Both routes became popular. 90,000 men came to California in 1849. Tens of thousands also came from Europe, South America, and China. In 1852, 20,000 came overland, 35,000 by sea. The state's population increased 25 times between 1848 and 1852. Women were scarce, only eight percent of the population in 1850.

Settlers had been coming overland since the early 1840s. The most popular route was the South Pass to Salt Lake, then across the desert and along the Humboldt River to California. The sea routes had great

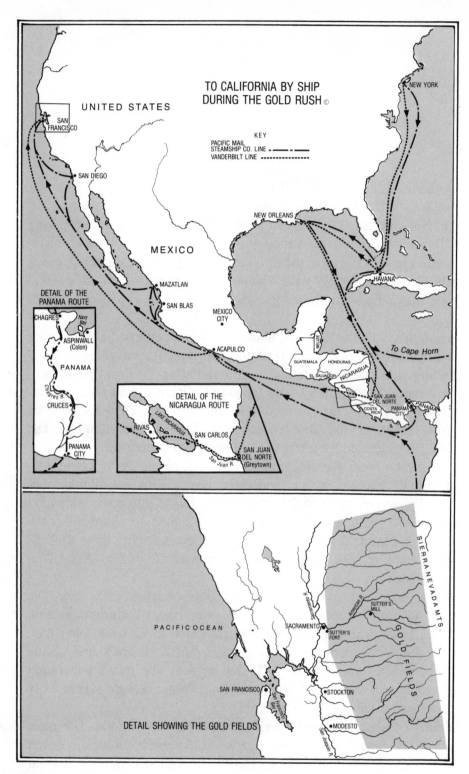

TO CALIFORNIA BY SHIP
DURING THE GOLD RUSH ©

KEY
PACIFIC MAIL
STEAMSHIP CO. LINE
VANDERBILT LINE

DETAIL OF THE PANAMA ROUTE

DETAIL OF THE NICARAGUA ROUTE

DETAIL SHOWING THE GOLD FIELDS

PER 1863 GOLDEN RULE CENTRAL AMERICAN TRANSIT Co

mand for ships was enormous. Every salvageable sailing hull was put back to sea. The whaling fleet converted for passengers.

The sea routes were through the Straits at Cape Horn, at the southern tip of South America, or to Panama, then overland to the Pacific Ocean and by ship north to San Francisco.

The Cape Horn route was 15,000 miles long, took 150-200 days and was dangerous. The east to west passage was very difficult because of the cold, unpredictable weather, storms, and treacherous currents. Not infrequently ships were wrecked or unable to make it through to the Pacific side. Even so, many went that way, enduring slippery decks, leaky cabins, rotten food, tropical heat and Antarctic cold. Stops to take on water, food, and wood were made at Havana, Rio de Janiero, Valparaiso in Chile, and the Galapagos Islands off Ecuador.

1850 GOLDEN GATE PACIFIC MAIL S.

The trans-Panama route became much more popular. It was only half the distance as around Cape Horn but it was hazardous also. The Isthmus of Panama was only 50 miles across and took five days to cross. From the Atlantic side the crossing was from Chagres or Porto Bello, up the Chagres River by canoe to the town of Cruces, then overland the final 20 miles by foot and mule to the Pacific Ocean at Panama City. This was the old Spanish trail, used to bring gold and silver from Peru to the Caribbean Sea for shipment to Spain. Most of it was in ruins from decades of disuse. Chagres was a dirty, primitive town of about 700 natives. The Indians extorted high fees for the river passage. There were no hotels to speak of anywhere. Sanitary conditions were terrible and cholera, yellow fever, malaria, and other tropical diseases were epidemic. As there was no effective treatment, cholera often killed its victims in a few days. Often the diseases were carried onto the ships on the Pacific side. The ship, *Uncle Sam*, arrived in San Francisco in 1855 with the worst-ever epidemic. 104 of the 650 passengers died of cholera on the trip.

Charles Nahl's 1868 picture "Incident On Chagres River" depicts the peril of travel on that river in Panama during the Gold Rush.

"Weapons Of The Argonauts" shows gold mining tools.

In 1847, before gold was discovered, Congress had appropriated funds to establish a regular mail service by steamer from the eastern United States to California and Oregon by way of Panama. The Atlantic ships, five steamers of about 1,000 tons, went from New York and Charleston or New Orleans. Three steamers operated on the Pacific side, making stops at Acapulco, San Blas, and Mazatlan, in Mexico.

The first steamship in this service, *California*, was 1050 tons with accommodations for 60 first class passengers and 150 steerage berths. She left New York on October 6, 1848 with only seven passengers. After clearing Cape Horn the ship picked up 150 Peruvians in Callao. But while she was en route, President Polk announced the California gold discovery, and at Panama City 1500 heavily armed Americans demanded passage to San Francisco. A near-riot developed. 350 passengers were taken. Upon arrival in San Francisco, on Febaruary 24, 1849, the crew promptly deserted to go to the gold fields. It took months to find a replacement crew for the ship's return voyage.

This became the story of the gold seekers. High hopes, great hazards, an uncertain journey whether by steamer or sailing ship.

Commodore Vanderbilt, the New York financier, sought improvements in the passage and in 1851 started a rival steamship line to Nicaragua, 500 miles north of Panama. The isthmus was 170 miles wide in Nicaragua, but most of it could be traveled by a small steamer across

103

SHIP: S. S. LEWIS
TYPE: Steamer   FROM: San Juan del Sur
ARRIVED: January 4, 1853   CAPTAIN: Sheppard
PASSAGE: 22 days from San Juan del Sur, Nicaragua, via
Acapulco, Mexico. Departed San Juan del sur on December
13, 1852 at 5:00PM and arrived at Acapulco on December 18,
1852 at 2:00AM. Had a constant succession of strong
breezes from the northwest, with weather very foggy. On
January 2, 1853, at 5:00PM, dropped anchor off the Heads,
too foggy to go in to San Francisco and out of coal. Sus-
tained damage on passage to San Francisco, broke shaft and
lay at anchor twenty-five miles from the city. Towed to
San Francisco by the steamer "Goliath".
   The "S.S. Lewis" arrived in San Francisco in a very
leaky condition, with several feet of water in her hold.
Visitors coming on board found her in a most filthy condition, one in which it was calculated to induce sickness
and death. Coupled with the fact that it had departed from
a notoriously unhealthy port, the arrival of the "S.S.
Lewis" resulted in a move to conduct an investigation.

   The below passengers died during the passage to San
Francisco:
No date of death-   W.H. Threkeld, of Missouri, buried
                     at Acapulco, Mexico
December 22, 1852-   William Shea, of Waukegen, Illinois,
                     of fever
December 24, 1852-   N. Elliott, of Toronto, Canada, of
                     diarrhea
December 25, 1852-   J. Sickels, of New York, of
                     diarrhea
December 27, 1852-   Joshua Kent, of Baltimore, Maryland,
                     aged 50, of diarrhea
December 30, 1852-   J. C. Greene, of Carlisle, Penn.,
                     aged 23, of diarrhea
                     A. Palow, Clayton, New York, of
                     diarrhea and fever, aged 47 years
December 31, 1852-   De Castro A. Putney /sic/, aged 30
                     years, of Brookfield, Wisconsin,
                     of fever and diarrhea
January 1, 1853-   Thomas Housely, of Lafayette County,
                     Wisconsin, aged 53, of fever and
                     diarrhea
                     Jacob Tsantree/sic/ (Trantree?), of
                     Wayne County, Ohio, aged 18 years
                     of fever and diarrhea
January 2, 1853-   William Grim, of Worcester, Wayne
                     County, Ohio, aged 45, of fever
                     and diarrhea

CARGO: Not listed.

Passengers

J.P. Winderly and lady
Mrs. __Madison and child
J.M. Jackson
Mrs. Hannah Hunt
W.B. Fleming and wife
J.P. Kirwan and wife
R.A. Bailey and wife
John J. Stettinius
Miss N.E. Young
E. Phithian, wife and child
J. Taylor
William Jones, wife and child
Mrs. __Yule
Samuel Thomson
Michael Roach
D. Parker
G.A. Miller, wife and child
Mrs. __Shepheard/sic/ and child
Miss Louisa Ball
Mrs. Sarah Stephenson and child
Mrs. S. Phillips and 2 childrn
H.S. Daniels, wife and 2 childrn
A. Underwood
F. Randall
S.B. Joslin
G.W. Bishop
E. Willie
Miss M. Walton
A.T. Land
O. McCracken
G. Lewis
J.S. Wilkinson
John Hammond

P. Gutshall and lady
N. C. Walton, lady and 3 childrn
L.F. Olds
J.O. Wiswall
C.P. Canfield
J.C. Rhodes
Mrs. M. Jab /sic/ and 2 childrn
Mrs. M.L. Buckner
H. Roland
Mrs. __McConu /sic/ (McConn?)
J. Levelling (?) (Leveling?), wife & 3 childrn
Eli Levelling /sic/
C.W. Nystron
Issac L. Stanton
William H. Scudder and wife
Mrs.__Weatherald
W.T. Head and
Mrs. Jane Webb
Mrs. Sarah Winters and 2 childrn
Mrs. __Yale and 3 childrn
George Hutchings and wife
Mrs.__Warner and two childrn
S.A. Barker, wife and child
E. Mendham /sic/
James Smith
J. Conway
J. Cave
W. Tholkeld /sic/
Mrs. E.A. Parker
W.R. Ferguson

Daniel O'Donnell
J. Smith
P.K. Sexton, lady and 4 childrn
S.S. Salsworth
A. Cameron
D.C. Anderson
C. Crippen, wife and 2 childrn
A.C. Hinkson
M.A. Baker, wife and child
H.A. Harris
R. King and wife
Mrs. __Sims and child
John D. McCowan
P.J. Glover
H.M. Densmore
A. Densmore
C.L. Newman, wife and 2 childrn
R.W. Turner, wife
Miss R.A. Turner
Rev. T. Butts
Charles Ash, wife and child
William Grim, wife and 3 childrn
E.P. Jackson
Mrs.__Hatch and child
F.M. Jones
George Givens
J. Bailey
J.B. Riddle
V.C. Ferguson
J.F. Gray
J.A. Dauis (?) (Dauit?)
George Connolly

and several unidentified in the steerage
- - - - - - -

Lake Nicaragua. Vanderbilt advertised this route as shorter, healthier, and more scenic. The price charged through Panama was slashed. Whether the route was an improvement is debatable. There was an epidemic of cholera in 1855. Vanderbilt enticed business back by cutting the first-class fare from New York to San Francisco to $180.00, $75.00 for steerage. First-class cabins had 2-4 berths; steerage contained 50 beds in a single room.

As early as 1848 American business interests had reached agreement with the local government to build a railroad across Panama. This was completed in 1855 and the running time from ocean to ocean was three to four hours, with a $25.00 fare. The railroad carried 30,000 passengers a year and the disease rate declined greatly.

A trans-Mexico route from Vera Cruz to Mazatlan existed for a few months in 1858 and 1859 but 100 miles in a bumpy stage coach made it unpopular.

The competition between the steamship lines was fierce. Many ships came to San Francisco, never to leave, left in the mud to become hotels, bars, restaurants, or business houses.

Ships crowd San Francisco Bay during the Gold Rush.

Courtesy National Maritime Museum, San Francisco.

In 1859 there was a new surge of traveling, when gold and silver were discovered in Nevada in the Comstock Lode.

The Pony Express began in 1860. Letters traveled from New York to Sacramento in 12 days, with a postal rate of $3.00 per half pound letter. This outclassed the steamers for quick mail delivery.

In 1869 the transcontinental railroad was completed. The fare to California was $173.00. Demand for ship travel to California collapsed.

The gold rush brought hundreds of thousands of people to California. Most of them didn't get rich digging gold. Some returned home empty-handed, and many died. Some went back deploring the change of life style they had seen. But San Francisco became a great city, with a spirit of adventure that has remained an essential part of California living.

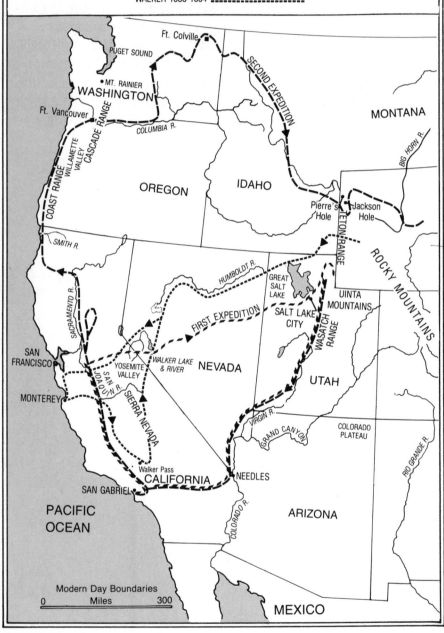

EARLY AMERICAN EXPLORERS
JEDEDIAH SMITH AND JOSEPH R. WALKER
REACH ALTA CALIFORNIA

KEY
SMITH: FIRST ROUTE, 1826-1827 – – – –
SECOND ROUTE, 1827-1829 – – –
WALKER 1833-1834 ·······

Ft. Colville

PUGET SOUND

MT. RAINIER

WASHINGTON

SECOND EXPEDITION

MONTANA

Ft. Vancouver

COLUMBIA R.

BIG HORN R.

WILLAMETTE VALLEY

CASCADE RANGE

COAST RANGE

OREGON

IDAHO

Pierre's Hole

Jackson Hole

SMITH R.

TETON RANGE

ROCKY MOUNTAINS

SACRAMENTO R.

HUMBOLDT R.

GREAT SALT LAKE

UINTA MOUNTAINS

FIRST EXPEDITION

SALT LAKE CITY

SAN FRANCISCO

YOSEMITE VALLEY

WALKER LAKE & RIVER

NEVADA

WASATCH RANGE

SAN JOAQUIN R.

MONTEREY

SIERRA NEVADA

UTAH

VIRGIN R.

GRAND CANYON

COLORADO PLATEAU

RIO GRANDE R.

Walker Pass

CALIFORNIA

NEEDLES

SAN GABRIEL

PACIFIC OCEAN

COLORADO R.

ARIZONA

Modern Day Boundaries
0   Miles   300

MEXICO

CHAPTER 13
OVERLAND TO CALIFORNIA
JEDEDIAH SMITH, JOHN MARSH, JOHN BIDWELL
THE DONNER PARTY

OVERLAND TRAVEL INTO CALIFORNIA came slowly. The Rockies and Sierras were formidable mountain barriers that secured the isolation of Mexican Alta California. The stories of some travelers to the region help to explain the difficulties involved.

Jedediah Smith

Jedediah Smith led the first party of Americans into Alta California in 1826. He was 27 years old. Smith had legendary courage and wilderness savvy. Unlike his boisterous companions with their long beards and drinking ways, he imagined himself as St. Paul, bringing Christianity to the frontier. He neither smoked, drank, nor slept with Indian women. He shaved every day and read the Bible each night by the light of the campfire.

Smith and his party of 17 beaver trappers were the first white men through the South Pass of the Rockies. They traveled on to the Great Salt Lake, then south through the Mohave Desert into southern California to the Mission San Gabriel, south of Los Angeles. From there Smith went to San Diego, to ask the Mexican governor, Echeandia, for permission to trap in California. Believing the band of buckskin clad men to be spies, Echeandia refused.

Smith promised to leave California and went north, looking for the fabled Buenventure River, thought to flow from the Great Salt Lake to the Pacific Ocean. A base camp was made on the Stanislaus River before an eastern crossing of the Sierras, made in only eight days, and the first time these mountains had ever been breached by white men.

Jedediah Smith's portrait recreated from a sketch done by a friend shortly after his death.

In Utah Smith met old partners, and together they returned to California by the previous route through the Mohave Desert. They were ambushed by Indians and ten of the eighteen men were killed. Smith reached his camp on the Stanislaus River but was captured and taken by Mexicans to jail in San Jose. Again Governor Echeandia refused him permission to remain in California.

Smith's party moved north into Oregon. The Smith River and Redwoods State Park in the region are named for him. While Jedediah Smith and two other trappers were out scouting, the rest of his party were killed by Indians. He escaped to safety at Fort Vancouver, then returned East. He had circled the West twice. In 1831, aged 32, he was killed by Comanche Indians in New Mexico.

Old Joe (Joseph R.) Walker

Old Joe Walker was a legendary frontier scout of the West, who managed to survive his daring exploits and die of natural causes. Working for the U.S. Army explorer, Captain Benjamin Bonneville, Walker led a band of about 50 Americans into California in 1833. They were the first to cross the central Sierras going east to west, and in the process were

John Marsh,
California's first physician

the first Americans to see Yosemite Valley. They proceeded on to Monterey, where they were given a hearty welcome by the Mexicans. On his return back East, Walker went farther south through the Tehachapi Mountains and discovered the pass named for him. He led another expedition to the West in 1843 and served as a scout for the Fremont expeditions of 1844 and 1845-46.

John Marsh

Greed was the great failing of John Marsh, who is credited with being California's first practicing physician. Born and raised in Massachusetts, he graduated from Phillips Academy and Harvard College. Marsh wanted to become a physician, but lacked the money to pay for a medical education. He took a job as a teacher in the elementary school at Fort Snelling in the Indian Territory of Minnesota. For two years, in his spare time, he studied with the local doctor.

Soon he became Sioux Indian Agent and hoped to save enough money to pay for medical school. But he fell in love with a beautiful Sioux halfbreed, whom he married, and they soon had a son. Marsh became allied secretly with the Sioux in their wars with the Sauk and Fox tribes.

111

Information he gave the Sioux helped them massacre eighteen of their enemies.

Marsh also sold rifles secretly to the Sioux. Chief Black Hawk and a force of Fox Indians vowed revenge on Marsh. His government ordered him arrested and Marsh fled with his family to Illinois, where his wife died in childbirth. Leaving his son with a friendly physician's family, Marsh decided to try his luck on the western frontier.

Marsh moved to Independence, Missouri, the edge of American civilization, the departure point for immigrants going West. There the road divided into the southern Santa Fe Trail or the northern Oregon Trail. John Marsh established a general store but was unsuccessful.

He decided to take the Santa Fe Trail to California. On the way Comanche Indians captured him. After he successfully removed an arrowhead from the chief's arm, they forced Marsh to live with them as a medicine man. He escaped and moved on to Santa Fe, where he learned Spanish.

In 1836 he reached Los Angeles. The village had a population of about 50. A doctor was badly needed. John Marsh was penniless but by producing his Harvard diploma, written in Latin, he convinced the Mexican authorities that he was a doctor. He set up a medical practice, taking hides as payment for services. In a year a warehouse was full of his unusual fees. Marsh then decided to cash in his hides and move north. He became a Mexican citizen, was baptised a Roman Catholic and purchased a ranch at the base of Mount Diablo, in present-day Contra Costa County. On this spread, which was nine miles across, he settled down to raising cattle and doctoring.

Marsh became a widely acclaimed doctor, his fame only exceeded by his fees. He would go anywhere in northern California, treating the humble and the mighty. Family members of General Vallejo and Thomas Larkin were treated with good results. Fees were collected usually by taking home a good number of a family's cattle.

For a visit lasting days Marsh might demand 300 cattle from a wealthy patient. Usually the fee was more like 50 head. Marsh drove them back to his ranch. His patients and their families were often unhappy with his demands. The mother of a child he treated for headaches was charged 50 cattle. She paid, but insisted on collecting back 25 cattle for laundering two of his shirts!

The doctor wrote letters to the East urging Americans to come to California. He even gave directions to his place and made the journey

A young John Bidwell.   *Nancy Kelsey in later life.*

sound no more difficult than a long walk that would take only a few days. Marsh had a way with words, he loved to read, and John Bidwell described him as the most literate man he'd ever known.

The first wagon train across the Sierras, the Bidwell-Bartleson Party, followed his rather vague directions in their trek from St. Louis, Missouri, to Marsh's ranch in California. When they arrived John Marsh celebrated the occasion by killing two pigs and giving each person a tortilla. The next day he was aghast at his generosity and, in something of a depression, resolved to recoup the approximatedly $100 spent for the celebration. Marsh rode off to the Mexican government offices in San Jose to get each man a passport, which he then tried to sell to them for cash or a promise to pay him $5.00 later. There were hard feelings when the immigrants learned that Marsh had gotten the passports for nothing.

John Marsh was a leader in encouraging American settlement of California, and when the war with Mexico came, in rallying support for the American cause.

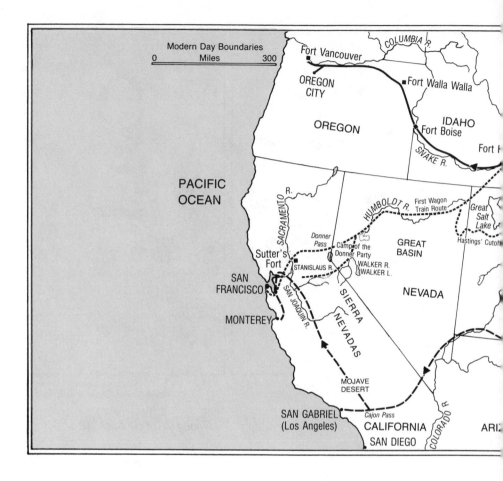

His fortunes continued to grow from his ranching, doctoring, and even his luck as a gold miner. Eventually he owned 50,000 acres of land, 6,000 cattle and 300 hogs.

On a trip to San Francisco in 1856 he was waylaid, robbed, and murdered by three of his vaqueros, who were disgruntled by his stingy payment for their work. His stone house still stands at the base of Mount Diablo.

John Bidwell

John Bidwell led the first overland immigrant train into California from the United States in 1841. A young school teacher, he decided to give up plans to go to a university and migrate to California. John Marsh's letters, published in local newspapers, were encouraging.

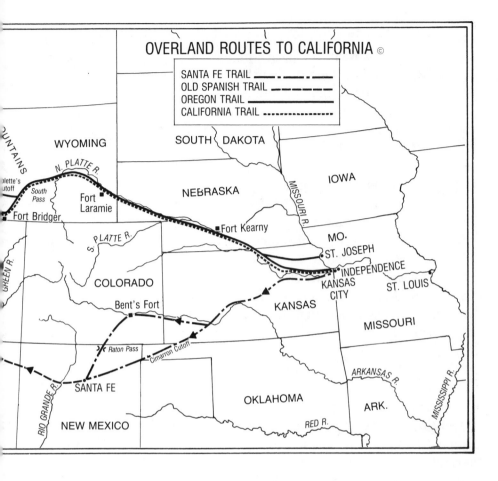

In 1840 in Missouri he discussed his plan with a French fur trapper named Rubidoux, who had actually gone there by the southern route through New Mexico and Arizona. Rubidoux described California in terms of everlasting Spring and orange trees. Bidwell organized a group of young men, women, and children for the trip. Some 69 people left St. Louis under the supposed direction of a Captain John Bartleson, but Bidwell became the actual leader.

The party had only indefinite directions. They followed the Platte River to Fort Laramie. In Wyoming the group separated with one band going north, eventually into Oregon. Bidwell's party, with 32 people accompanying him, went on past the Great Salt Lake into Nevada. They found the Walker River, then a stream that led into the Stanislaus River. The Sierras were probably crossed through Ebbett's Pass, south of Lake Tahoe. The 24 week trip that ended in November was harrowing. The

115

mules had to be killed for food and the wagons abandoned. The party arrived at the Los Medanos Ranch of John Marsh with little more than their tattered clothes. One of their hardy band was 17 year old Nancy Kelsey, who brought along her infant child.

John Bidwell became rich in California. He worked for John Sutter for several years, then became a naturalized Mexican citizen and received a land grant. During the war with Mexico he served as an officer in Fremont's California Battalion and drew up the American resolution of independence from Mexico.

During the Gold Rush he made a fortune mining, then bought the 22,000 acre Chino Ranch, which busied him for the rest of his life, experimenting with growing different crops. He founded the city of Chico and gave the State land to establish Chico Normal School, now Chico State University. John Bidwell lost three elections for Governor of California, but was a U.S. Congressman from 1865-67. In 1892 he was the Prohibition Party's candidate for U.S. President. A very correct man, someone said he was "too good to be Governor".

The Donner Party

The Donner Party experienced all the possible horrors of overland travel through the mountains of California in winter. Led by the two Donner families from Illinois, the 87 men, women, and children left Independence, Missouri in May of 1846, the last emigrant party of the year. They were caught in the Sierra snows in November, and the last were not rescued until April of 1847. 47 survived the cold and starvation. Their plight came from poor planning, weak leadership, and bad luck. They are remembered so well because some survivors resorted to cannibalism.

The complicated strand of misfortunes began with the decision to take a new route south of the Great Salt Lake, touted by a man named Lansford Hastings. The Donners were impressed by his claims, since he had written a book on the subject. The route was supposed to shorten the distance to California by 250 miles and their train was already behind schedule. Hastings actually knew nothing about the territory described and only hoped to make some money acting as a guide and by having friends sell supplies. The party became trapped in a difficult stretch of desert and mountain canyons, which slowed them so much that they could only travel 36 miles in 21 days.

116

Their best leader, James Reed, trying to hurry the pace, became involved in a quarrel with one of the team drivers. This ended with Reed killing a man who attacked Reed and his wife. The group held an impromptu trial and banished Reed from the party. Reed went ahead alone, reached Sutter's Fort in November, and tried unsuccessfully to reach the party through the snows, which came a month early that year.

The Donner Party arrived at what is now called Donner Lake in early November. Civilization, represented by Sutter's Fort, was 100 miles further west. They were unable to cross over the summit and became snowbound by an unusually severe winter. The snow was 30 feet deep. Totally inexperienced in what faced them, they quickly ran out of food, lost their remaining cattle in the snow, and were unable to find additional food. They settled into makeshift cabins near Donner Lake and nearby Alder Creek.

Their scraps of food soon disappeared and the living began eating those who had starved to death. Two attempts were made to get over the summit in November but the snow was already too deep. Four died in

A rescue of the Donner Party from an 1880 history of Nevada County, California.

Courtesy Bancroft Library, University of California, Berkeley.

117

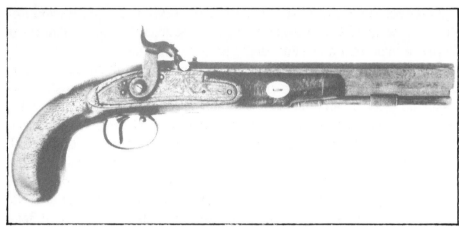

Jedediah Smith's pistol taken from his body when he was killed.

late December. On December 16th, seventeen began the ascent over the summit, using snowshoes made from the bows of oxen yokes lashed with thongs. Will Eddy, almost frozen, staggered into the first ranch on the west side of the summit, where a relief party had been organized. The relief party found fifteen survivers of the snowshoe group. Their escape effort had taken them a month.

On January 31 a relief party of seven men left Sutter's Fort. It reached Donner Lake on February 27 and took out 27 people. Another relief party led by James Reed left the fort February 7 and arrived at the lake on March 1 to take more survivers.

A final monstrous act was the probable murder of Mrs. Tamsen Donner by Lewis Keseberg. When the third relief party arrived, he was found eating her. He had lost his wife and two children. Keseberg was thought to have murdered Tamsen Donner for the $1500 she supposedly had. This Keseberg denied, claiming the $250 found on him was his wife's money. He was the last survivor, brought out in late April and forced to follow behind the group in disgrace.

Keseberg became the scapegoat of the whole incredible tragedy. It was never proved that he had murdered Tamsen Donner or robbed her. Shortly thereafter he sued one of his rescuers for slandering his name. He won the suit, but the judge awarded Keseberg only $1.00, and ordered him to pay the trial costs.

Keseberg remained an outcast. He never admitted any wrongdoing. Bad luck plagued his remaining years. He remarried, but his new wife died, leaving him with two mentally retarded children.

The murderer, James Reed, became a respected, admired, and rich man.

The conduct of the Donner Party is debated to this day. Mostly the verdict has been regretful acceptance of the cannibalism in this unprecedented ordeal. The story of the Donner Party lives on as a black legend in California history.

Soon the wagon trains came to California in a continuous, bone-jolting and difficult stream. But not overly dangerous for the time. In 1849 about 5,000 wagons came to the new territory. Most of these people were not frontiersmen, but former clerks, farmers, housewives, children, and other ordinary folk. Many planned badly, and the road from Missouri was littered with discarded organs and anvils too heavy to lug to their destination. Cholera and other diseases were a serious problem but the Indians weren't the anticipated danger. Most immigrants arrived with little more than they could carry. Still, the pressure was there to walk in to cheap land, a mild climate, a new start, and perhaps a fortune, in the Golden State.

CHAPTER 14
HISPANICS AND ANGLOS
HAVE AN UNSTEADY RELATIONSHIP
IN CALIFORNIA.
General Mariano G. Vallejo, Cesar Chavez

WHEN THE FIRST AMERICAN OVERLAND PARTY arrived in California in 1841, the leader, John Bidwell, estimated there were fewer than 100 non-Mexican settlers or Anglos (non-Hispanics) in the region. The Mexicans numbered about 7,000. Both groups were greatly outnumbered by the Indians, who had become more rebellious and were raiding the established settlements.

The government in Mexico did almost nothing to help their citizens in California. The soldiers and missionaries were not sent their pay from Mexico City. No one wanted to settle in California. Some prisoners from Mexico were sent as colonists over the objections of the established residents. Indian raids on isolated ranchos forced many settlers to abandon their property. As war with the United States approached, many were inclined to welcome a new strong government that might bring order and prosperity.

The peace treaty with Mexico agreed to respect the property rights of Mexican Californians, and after a year they could become U. S. citizens. For numerous reasons land ownership of the old ranchos soon eroded. Disputes were settled by a Land Commission that met in San Francisco, but it was difficult and expensive to get witnesses and attorneys to the hearings, especially from southern California. Often boundaries were hard to establish.

Drought, mismanagement, and other misfortunes made many land owners short of cash. The Gold Rush brought an army of American squatters. For a few years they profited from the miner's willingness to pay high prices for beef. Property taxes added to the demise of the great

*Mariano Vallejo
is his agreeable self.*

land holders. In southern California, where only 50 families owned the land, they hung on for a generation longer, but by 1880 most of the old Mexican-California way-of-life was over.

Many Mexicans and South Americans came to the gold fields, but they were disliked by Americans, who called them 'greasers' and harrassed them in every possible way.

A new era for Mexicans began when farm laborers were needed in the emerging new style of California agriculture. Before 1887 only 12,000 Mexicans lived in Southern California, but that year 120,000 Anglos came in by the railroad, making Mexicans an instant minority. Needed then as a seasonal work force, Mexicans were welcome only part of the year.

In the early days of this century there were almost no attempts to control the movements of Mexicans back and forth across the border. The Mexican government aggravated the exodus of its citizens to the United States by encouraging European immigration into Mexico, promising land formerly farmed by Mexicans to the newcomers. In 1917 the U. S. devised special immigration rules, admitting 'temporary' farm workers, railroad maintainence workers, and miners. It is estimated that most of the temporary workers never returned to Mexico.

General Mariano Vallejo relaxes on the lawn of his Sonoma home.

By the 1920's Mexicans supplied most of California's farm labor. During the 1930's they were partially replaced by Okies, but since then Mexicans have been on the bottom rung of the California labor market.

Contrary to popular belief, Hispanics have mostly become city dwellers. By 1950 only a third of them lived in rural areas. By 1980, 90% lived in cities. A high birth rate in Mexico and Central America, combined with high unemployment and poverty, has made the U.S. an irresistible magnet. In 1980, 4,544,331 people or 19% of California's total population, were of Hispanic origin. Over 40% of them were from Mexico. Estimates are that in 1990 approximately 25% of the state's 28 million total population will be Hispanic. By 2020 it is estimated the state will be 38% Hispanic.

A landmark immigration bill passed by Congress in 1986 made it possible for illegal aliens to gain citizenship if they could prove residence in the U.S. since 1981. Hispanics could benefit from many provisions of the new law.

California, the state with the largest economy, will continue to be a refuge for the poor of Latin America. Revolutions and depressed economic conditions push people north. Unlike most of the ethnic groups in California, Hispanic voyagers may have only just begun arriving at our shores.

General Mariano G. Vallejo

Mariano G. Vallejo was an outstanding figure in both Mexican Alta California and American California, but he also reflects many attitudes in that transition period between them. Although born in California, he became a voyager to the new state, by adopting its cause and taking U. S. citizenship.

Born in Monterey, Vallejo took up soldiering at age 15 and was a soldier in the Mexican government in California until the U. S. conquest. As an officer and career soldier he fought Indians and protected the northern reaches of Mexican California. In 1832 he married Francisca Benicia Carrillo, a daughter of one of Alta California's most influential families. They had sixteen children.

Vallejo's nephew, Juan Bautista Alvarado, sent the Mexican officials home in 1836 and established an independent California. Mariano Vallejo was appointed military commander of the northern territory. Mexico reestablished its authority in 1842 and Vallejo continued in his powerful position. He became the most influential figure in northern California and owned huge land holdings near present-day Vallejo, Sonoma, Benicia, and Petaluma.

At the outbreak of the Bear Flag Revolt in 1846, Vallejo and his brother Salvador were arrested by the Americans and jailed for two months at Sutter's Fort. The arrest came after a night of hospitality shown to the Americans by Vallejo. William B. Ide, who was present and became the republic's President, said, "the richest wines and brandies sparkled in the glasses, and those who had thus unceremoniously met soon become merry companions; more especially the weary visitors, and the bottles had well nigh vanquished the captors." Even so, General Vallejo went off to jail. All along he was sympathetic to the American cause.

After the war Vallejo continued living on his estates and in his home in Sonoma, named Lachryma Montis ("Tear of the Mountain"). He welcomed making California part of the United States, was elected to the state's Constitutional Convention and served in California's first Senate. The city of Vallejo was begun on his land. He tried to have the state

*Cesar Chavez
speaking to a
meeting of farm
workers in Salinas
in 1985.*

capitol located in either Vallejo or Benicia, but after brief trials both sites were abandoned, and Sacramento was selected. His old rancho at Petaluma is now a state park.

Vallejo, an agreeable, capable and discerning man, finished his long life as a revered figure in Sonoma. His name is memorable in California's history.

Cesar Chavez

In a 1984 *Los Angeles Times* poll, Cesar Chavez was named by other Hispanics as the most admired Hispanic in California. He received twice as many votes as the next two favorites—movie and TV star Ricardo Montalban, and ace Los Angeles pitcher, Fernando Valenzuela.

Chavez became famous for organizing farm workers in the Central Valley in the 1960's and 1970's. His parents were Mexicans who migrated first to Arizona, where Cesar was born. For a time the family owned a farm near Yuma. They were evicted for unpaid taxes and water bills in 1937 when he was 10.

The family began following the crop harvests in California, living the life of destitute migrant farm workers. Cesar did this work for years, married, and eventually settled in San Jose. For ten years he worked as a union organizer for the Community Service Organization, which served the needs of Hispanics in California and Arizona. In 1962 he resigned to devote his energies to the organization of a union for agricultural workers. He was 35 when he founded the Farm Workers Association. Later this became the United Farm Workers, which he continues to head.

The short, unimposing figure began to organize the grape workers in the Delano area. The inner strength of his convictions proved to be a match for the powerful wealthy growers and conservative politicians. Fighting for higher wages, better working conditions, and union recognition he lead his workers into a prolonged strike. The seventh grade drop-out quoted Gandhi and St. Paul, lead a march on the State capitol, organized national boycotts of the growers' grapes, and finally had his union accepted in 1970. Cesar Chavez became a national labor hero, esteemed by the likes of governors and senators. After doing battle for five years the struggle seemed over.

Critics claim that Chavez and the union have lost their way, that "La causa" lacks vitality. The United Farm Workers represents fewer workers and the average wage is little more than it was in 1970. Still, Cesar Chavez symbolizes for Hispanics the hope of a better life.

CHAPTER 15
THE ENGLISH AND SCOTS IN EARLY CALIFORNIA
William A. Richardson, Andrew S. Hallidie, John Muir

PEOPLE WITH ORIGINS IN THE BRITISH ISLES were the dominant group in the Americanization of California. Their influence was so pervasive that they formed the background against which other national groups stood out. There were many nationalities represented in settled East Coast America, but most of the people had come from Britain. Once Americans began to pour into California during the Gold Rush, the Anglo-Saxon influence became overwhelming. Aside from this indirect English influence, there was heavy immigration from England and Scotland, as well as Ireland.

Of course, the first Englishmen were with Francis Drake in 1579, even before the earliest English colony at Jamestown in Virginia, in 1607. But because England was unable to enforce Drake's claim to "New Albion," English influence in California disappeared until the late 1700's and early 1800's. Then English ships began appearing on the California coast, wanting to trade with the Mexicans and Russians.

In 1792 and 1794 Captain George Vancouver visited the Spanish settlements at San Francisco and Monterey. As the Spanish had only puny forces, Vancouver suggested to his government that California might be a good place to relocate some of England's poor.

Located to the north in Canada, England coveted California until the Americans overran it during the Gold Rush and settled the issue. Although California didn't become English, many British subjects were important in the state's development.

John Gilroy, a Scotch sailor, jumped ship in 1814 and became the first permanent foreign resident in California. William A. Richardson and Robert Livermore were English sailors who left their ships and remained in California. They both became wealthy by acquiring huge

Captain William A. Richardson with his mariner's telescope.

Courtesy Kelley House Museum, Mendocino.

land grants from the Mexican government. Both took Mexican wives and adapted to the California scene.

Livermore ran away to sea at age 16. In 1822 he deserted his ship in Monterey , learned Spanish, and worked for ranchers hunting down Indian horse thieves. He formed a lifelong partnership with his friend, Jose Noriega. They built a house together in the Sunol Valley and began raising cattle. In 1838 he married Josepha Higuerra, a widow from a prominent ranching family. By then he owned 3,000 cattle spread over his Las Positas Rancho near present-day Livermore. Eventually he and Noriega owned over 26,000 acres. He lived in a grand style in the Spanish manner.

William A. Richardson

When he was 27, in 1822, William Richardson asked for permission to leave his ship, the British whaler Orion, at the Presidio in San Francisco . The request was made in writing to Governor Pablo Vincent de

A cable car climbs a San Francisco hill in the 1870s.

Sola. The governor wrote on the margin, "Being aware that the petitioner, besides being a navagator, is conversant with and engaged in the occupation of a carpenter. I hereby grant the privilege he asks for, with the obligation that he shall receive and teach such young men as may be placed in his charge by my successor."

The story is that when he got off his ship one of the daughters of the Commandante, Maria Antonia Martinez, vowed she would marry the handsome sailor, which is what happened. As required, Richardson became a Mexican citizen and was baptized a Catholic. He also took part of her name—Antonio. They had three children and apparently were very happy together.

Immediately Richardson built himself a launch and a small sailing vessel. With Indian crews he began to bring in produce from the neighboring mission gardens. He sailed to Sitka, Alaska, and Peru on trading voyages. Later he and his family moved to Mission San Gabriel near Los Angeles. In 1835 he met Governor Figueroa and asked permission to build a commercial town at Yerba Buena Cove in San Francisco Bay.

Richard H. Dana, author of **Two Years Before The Mast**, visited Yerba Buena in 1835 and described Richardson as the only non-Mexican to be found there.

The English sailor became Captain of the Port from 1835 to 1844. Members of his family were the first residents of Yerba Buena, which became San Francisco in 1847. He was rewarded with valuable land grants. His Rancho Sauselito (spelled differently from the present spelling) in Marin County, acquired in 1838, now includes Sausalito, Stinson Beach, and Muir Woods. Richardson's Bay was named after him. In 1844, for unpaid back wages, he was given the Albion Grant on the Mendocino Coast, between the present towns of Mendocino and Manchester. This claim was later invalidated in the U.S. courts.

Richardson was an important and unusual man in early California history.

Andrew S. Hallidie

Andrew Smith Hallidie was 16 when he arrived in California in 1852. He was born in London into a prominent family. The name Hallidie was added to his family name of Smith in honor of an uncle and godfather,

*A formal painted portrait
of Andrew Smith Hallidie.*

Courtesy Bancroft Library,
University of California, Berkeley.

who was court physician to both King William IV and Queen Victoria. The family came to California to operate a ranch in Mariposa County, but Andrew's father quickly lost interest in ranching and returned to England. Andrew decided to stay.

For a time he tried mining for gold but soon became interested in the mechanics of mining. He devised a method to make cables by twisting steel wires together. These were used to build suspension bridges over rivers and to haul buckets of ore down mountain sides. In 1865 he formed a company to make this wire rope, which was in great demand in the silver mines of Nevada. Two years later he invented an endless cable for mining.

Hallidie is best remembered for conceiving and building the San Francisco cable car system. He placed his continuous cable in a slot in the ground, and the cars moved by clamping onto the cable, which was pulled by a steam engine. The inventor said the idea came to him while watching horses strain in pulling street cars up the steep San Francisco hills. The first cable cars began to run in 1873 and continue to this day. The system was soon used in other cities.

An intellectual man, Andrew Hallidie helped draw up the first charter for the City and County of San Francisco. He was appointed to the first Board of Regents of the University of California in 1868 and served on that body until his death in 1900. Hallidie Plaza, near the start of the first cable car line on Powell Street, honors his name.

John Muir

John Muir, no doubt, is the most beloved Scot to leave his mark on California. He was born in 1838 in Dunbar, Scotland, one of six children. In 1849 his father decided to move to America, to Wisconsin, where he bought a farm. There the family settled into a life of unceasing work under the stern rule of their incredibly pious father. The only time John was allowed for himself was before the work day, which began at 4:00 a.m. He would wake himself at 1:00 a.m. to have time to read. His father thought the only book worth reading was the Bible.

John was bright and inventive. He became something of a celebrity by building amusing contraptions, such as a wooden alarm clock that activated a device to tip the user out of bed in the morning. In 1860 he went off to the University of Wisconsin, hoping to become a physician. The terrible battles of the Civil War soon cast a gloomy pall over the country. John Muir had strong pacifist convictions. He also had a difficult time financing his studies.

In 1864 he took a job as a mechanic in a Canadian sawmill, where his brother was working. He devised a machine that could make 2,500 rake handles a day. A strong interest in the outdoors and botany began to appear. The next year he decided to move on, to Indianapolis, Indiana, where he worked as a factory mechanic making wagon wheels. Then he had an accident that changed his life. A file slipped and struck his eye. Soon Muir lost the sight of both eyes. Gradually, after several weeks, his sight returned. His employers valued his inventive abilities and offered to make him a partner in the firm. But John decided the commercial world was not for him.

He wanted to see the world—the Amazon, Alaska, California. This desire resulted in a walking trek to Florida, and was the subject of a later book, **A Thousand-Mile Walk to the Gulf.** In Havana, Cuba, he decided to go to California instead of the Amazon and arrived in San Francisco in March, 1868. Almost immediately he set off walking to Yosemite Valley. Throughout his life he was a great hiker, and thought nothing of walking hundreds of miles with only a change of underclothes, a knife, matches, and the simplest equipment.

Muir stayed in the Sierras for five years, supporting himself as a shepherd and saw mill operator. He exulted in the seasons, the storms, and the mysteries of the creation of that beautiful place. He developed a theory that the Yosemite Valley had been quarried by an ancient glacier, instead of being pushed up by earthquakes.

In 1871 he sold his first essay, "Yosemite Glaciers", to the *New York Tribune.* He had become a nature writer. Many books and articles followed about his experiences. John Muir became one of the nation's best read and respected authors on the outdoors and the growing conservation movement. There were many journeys in California and to every continent in the world.

Not until he was 40 did he marry. His wife was the daughter of a rancher and physician who lived near Martinez. Muir settled into running the ranch. For ten years he attended to business and became independently wealthy. Then the urge to roam reappeared. His wife understood. Confinement seemed to make him ill with indigestion and bronchitis. The outdoors restored his appetite and vigor.

In 1888 he began to write again and took a camping trip to the glaciers of Alaska. He lobbied Congress to protect some of his Sierra

A close-up of John Muir.

*President Theodore Roosevelt
and John Muir pose together
at Yosemite National Park in 1903.*

haunts by making them National Parks. Yosemite had long been a state park, but Muir felt that it would be protected better by the federal government. He was asked to draw up the map for its boundaries. In 1890, Congress passed the laws establishing Yosemite, Sequoia, and General Grant National Park (which later became part of Kings Canyon National Park).

In 1892, with some friends, he established the Sierra Club for "preserving the forests and other natural features of the Sierra Nevada Mountains." He served as the president of this powerful environmentalist group until his death in 1914.

John Muir became the friend of several U.S. Presidents. In 1903 he spent four days with President Theodore Roosevelt in Yosemite. Roosevelt later doubled the number of national parks and put an additional 148,000,000 acres of forest into reserves.

Muir's greatest disappointment was his failure to protect Hetch

Hetchy Valley, behind Yosemite, which was dammed and obliterated to become a water source for San Francisco. He felt the purpose could have been met by other means without destroying the beautiful valley. It was one of the few defeats this splendid man ever incurred.

Many places have been named in his honor, including a mountain in California, a glacier in Alaska, and the magnificent Muir Woods National Monument in Marin County.

CHAPTER 16
THE SONS OF EIRE IN DEVELOPING CALIFORNIA
Sam Brannan's Story

ENGLAND RULED IRELAND (EIRE) for 700 years before the establishment of the Irish Free State in 1922. The woes of Ireland are legendary. English rule was harsh. The British aristocracy owned almost all the land, and the Irish were reduced to peasant renters. Most of the land owners lived in Britain, and some never visited their estates during their lifetime.

The Irish Penal Code, put into effect in 1691, survived for 125 years and gave the Irish almost no civil rights. They were not allowed to vote, serve on a jury, enter the armed forces, teach school, become lawyers, enter a university, or work for the government. Often even trivial criminal offenses were punished by hanging. These laws were eased somewhat in the 1700's, but continued English domination and oppressive economic conditions made immigration to America, and later to California, a godsend.

In the years just before the American Revolution the desertion of the mother country reached proportions alarming to the establishment. "Rack-renting," a common practice of the landlord, raised the rent with every improvement made by the tenant. The Industrial Revolution passed Ireland by. In the 1770's foreign purchases of Irish linen diminished, drastically affecting the Irish economy. The price of bread rose to levels that threatened famine. Cheap food, plenty of work, and the chance to escape these troubles produced a flood of immigration to America.

In 1846 and 1847 an even worse disaster struck—a blight afflicted potatoes, a staple of the Irish diet. The potatoes seemed to rot in the ground. No one understood the viral cause or knew what to do. By 1847 half a million people had starved to death. This new reason for immigration coincided with the California Gold Rush.

In America the Irish followed new patterns by becoming city dwellers instead of farmers. They showed an aptitude for government, and many became prominent politicians. This was probably helped along by their traditional esteem for those with the gift of story telling and oratory. The Irish flair for hilarity, self-deprecation, goodfellowship, and the cheerful sufferance of adversity, all helped. English was their first language, as the use of Gaelic had been suppressed in Ireland. They fit in quickly, especially in California, where background was of little importance. In the East they filled the tenements and were relegated to the status of uneducated laborers and servants. In California they were what they could convince others they could be.

In 1848 the population of California was about 15,000, not counting native Indians. About 7,000 were Mexicans and about 6,000 were Americans who had moved in. The rest were from all over the world. The Gold Rush caused a great influx of foreigners as well as Americans. Domestic migration from eastern United States continued to account for most of the new residents. The main source of foreigners was England and Ireland. By 1860 about a fifth of the state's 146,000 foreign-born were counted as Irish. In the 1870's 30 percent of the state's population was of domestic or immigrant Irish background. After that the proportion declined, but it has continued to be considerable.

There have been many influential California Irishmen. A few, like Timothy Murphy, John Read, and James Richard Berry, had Mexican land grants in Marin County. Jasper O'Farrell was the Surveyor-General of Alta California.

During the Gold Rush not many made fortunes in the California mines, but some did strike it big in Nevada. In 1859 two Irish miners, Peter O'Riley and Patrick McLaughlin, working their gold claims in western Nevada, discovered the Comstock Lode, near present day Virginia City. It proved to be an incredibly rich deposit of both silver and gold. In 1873 John Mackay and James Fair discovered the biggest trove of all nearby, the Bonanza Mine. $190,000,000 worth of gold and silver was taken out. Mackay and Fair, with two other Irishmen, James C. Flood and William G. O'Brien, became the "Silver Kings" of the Comstock Lode.

Some made money in business ventures, although Irishmen brought no financial experience to America. Peter Donahue organized the company that created San Francisco's first gas lighting system. He made so much money that he could give his wife a carriage made of glass, like

Cinderella. Edward Martin organized the Hibernia Bank. But most Irish were involved in more modest businesses. There was plenty of drinking in California, and some became the premier saloon keepers, as well as policemen, in the rowdy new cities.

After the transcontinental railroad was finished in 1869 there was a great surplus of workers in California. The Irish had supplied most of the labor on the tracks coming west and many of the men continued on to California. Times were hard. The Chinese were blamed. Denis Kearney, a sailor from Ireland, had settled in San Francisco in 1877 and became the spokesman for resentful white laborers. His speeches, usually given in vacant lots, always ended with: "The Chinese must go!" Kearney established the Workingman's Party and scored a landslide victory in 1879. But people finally tired of his simplistic rhetoric, and he lost influence. In 1884 he retired from politics and became a real estate salesman.

*U. S. Senator from California
David Broderick,
killed in a duel over slavery
in 1857.*

136

Other prominent early California Irish politicians and businessmen were David Broderick, John G. Downey, and James Phelan. David Broderick immigrated from Kilkenny. After running a saloon he came to California in the Gold Rush. He read law, became an attorney, and was elected to the state Senate. Before the Civil War he became a leading figure in the state Democratic Party opposing slavery. Then he was elected to the U.S. Senate, where he was challenged to a duel by a slavery advocate. At the time a politician could not hope to refuse a duel and keep his honor and influence. Most such duels were shams, and Broderick fired his shot into the ground. His opponent shot Broderick just below the heart and killed him.

John G. Downey became the State's seventh governor during the Civil War. He was an immigrant from Ireland who had arrived in California with $10.00. Thirteen years after opening the first drug store in Los Angeles, he was elected governor.

James Phelan, also an immigrant, was a grocery clerk in New York before coming to California during the Gold Rush. He opened a saloon, successfully sold real estate, then started his own bank. He became a reform mayor of San Francisco, and a U. S. senator.

*Sam Brannan,
who established many firsts
in California history.*

The California Star.

VOL. 1.   YERBA BUENA, JANUARY 9, 1847   **NO. 1.**

THE CALIFORNIA STAR.
A WEEKLY JOURNAL,
Devoted to the Liberties and Interests of the
People of California.
Published by Samuel Brannan.
Edited by E. P. Jones.

TERMS.
IVARIABLY IN ADVANCE

One copy per annum, · · · · Cash $6,00
Two copies,   " · · · · " 10,00

ADVERTISEMENTS.

One square, (10 lines) 2 insertions, $3,00, and $1 for every additional insertion. One half square or less, 2 insertions, $2,00, and 75 cts for every additional insertion. For yearly advertising apply to the Publisher.

LATER FROM THE
ARMY.
PROGRESS OF THE WAR.
MATAMORAS TAKEN WITHOUT OPPOSITION.
Mexican Soldiers Deserting in Great Numbers.
Additional Particulars of the Actions OF THE 8th AND 9th.

The Electric Telegraph at Jersey City communicates the following important and interesting intelligence from the seat of war.

From the New Orleans Delta, May 29.

The Steam Ship Telegraph has arrived from Point Isabel. Through the politeness of her obliging clerk we have been furnished with the following information:—

He reports that on the 17th instant, a detachment of 300 regulars and 350 volunteers proceeded to Barita and took possession of it, and established a military depot.

On the morning of the 19th, an express arrived from Gen. Taylor, stating that he had crossed the Rio Grande and taken the City of Matamoras without opposition.

The Mexicans have fled the city—the Mexicans from the last accounts were deserting their ranks in battalions?

Two regiments, with the exception of about 350, having marched a few days previous, were stationed at Brazos Point awaiting the orders of Gen. Taylor, as it was thought they would leave on the 20th for Matamoras, via the old Barita road.

Col. McIntosh, Capt. Page, and all the others who were wounded in the action of the 8th and 9th, are at Point Isabel, and are recovering.

The Telegraph is just 26 hours from Point Isabel. Capt. Auld, of the Telegraph, who has had opportunities for obtaining correct information has given us some interesting particulars in relation to our army operations.

We have now scarcely time to allude to them. The escape of Capt. Thornton, at the time his company was so badly cut up, is almost incredible.

After carrying him safely over a high hedge, enclosing which he had been decoyed, his horse brought him safely over fences and deep ravines, swimming the Rio Grande above Matamoras.

Then passing down below the town on the opposite side, in attempting to leap a broad ditch he missed his footing, when both horse and rider were thrown by the fall. The Capt. was so stunned that he was soon after taken up by the Mexicans perfectly uncentious of what had happened.

After the battle of the 8th, he was exchanged and restored to our army.

Capt. Auld thinks the whole number of our killed and wounded must amount to more than 300. Besides the wounded taken to St. Josephs, there are now 40 at Point Isabel too badly wounded to be removed. All but three it is thought will recover.

The condition of the brave and esteemed Capt. Page is melancholly indeed; the whole of his lower jaw, with part of his tongue and palate was shot away by a grape shot.

He, however, survived, though entirely incapable of speech, only communicating his thoughts by writing on a slate, and receiving the necessary nutriment for the support of life with much difficulty.

He does not desire to live, but converses with cheerfulness and exultation upon the success of our army.

All our accounts represent the Mexicans as having fought on the 8th and 9th with the courage and desperation which would have reflected credit upon the troops of any nation.

They were nearly in a state of starvation, and had been promised the ample supplies of the American camp in case they should secure the victory.

They met the charge of our troops manfully, and stood the destructive fire that was pouring in upon them without giving way, until the works were encumbered with the dead and wounded.

The thunder storms of last night, between this city and Baltimore, interrupted the Telegraph, otherwise the above intelligence would have been here some hours earlier.

Treatment of American Prisoners by the Mexicans.

Capt. Hardee, who was taken prisoner in the capture of Thornton's company, states, in a letter to a friend in Savannah, that they were treated with the greatest consideration and kindness. Gen. Arista received the prisoners in the most gracious manner, and said that "his nation had been regarded as barbarous, and that he wished to prove to them the contrary." Capt. Hardee says: "Lieut. Kane and myself are living with Gen. Ampudia, lodge in his hotel and sit at his table. We are not on parole, but in company with one of the General's aids—go pretty much where and when we please. Two of his aids speak excellent English, and the General himself speaks French, so that we are admirably off in this respect. Every one around us use their utmost endeavours to make our time pass pleasantly, and if any thing could make us forget our captivity it would be the frank and agreeable manners and generous hospitality of Gen Ampudia. He and General Arista are both men of high tone and character." These facts are highly honorable to the Mexicans.

Mexican Affairs.

The Washington Correspondent of the Journal of Commerce says:

"We are anxiously expecting intelligence from the Army of occupation. The news will, it is thought, determine the question whether we are to have a long war or a short one.

'Mexico is probably well acquainted, by this time, with the disposition of the British government towards this quarrel; and if she is to have no help from that quarter, then she might as well negotiate at once.

'The Mexican Government would not venture upon a war with the United States without the belief that it would have foreign support.

'At the time when, by the intervention of France and Great Britan, the Mexican Government was induced to recognize the independence

of Texas, for the purpose of defeating anexation, a pledge was given by the English and French Ministers, that if the project should fail, Mexico should have aid in resenting the injury of which she complained. That these Ministers did not give this assurance without authority, may be readily conjectured, after the disclosures which have been made by M. Guizot and the London 'Times'

'That Mexico has apprehended, and with good reason too, the loss of California, in the case of a war is very certain; and it is not probable that she refused negotiation before she had been assured that the integrity of her territory should be maintained by France and Great Britain. We shall soon see how this matter is. If the principle posts of California have not already been taken by our squadron, they will be in less than thirty days from this time; and they will be held too, until the war is ended, and its expenses paid by Mexico."

Annexation.

It appears from the latest papers from the United States, that information had been received at New Orleans and Havana, which was relied upon as correct, that thirteen of the Mexican Provinces had notified the leaders of the party in power in that ill fated country of their determination not to have anything to do with the present war with the United States, and that, unless certain demands, the particulars of which had not transpired, were complied with, they would immediately apply to the Government of the United States for admission into the Union. All the Provinces adjoining the State of Texas, are among the number mentioned. Tobasco has under Gen. Bruno raised the standard of revolt. It seems however from the following article from the New York "Sun," that Yucatan has taken a more decided stand than any of them.

By the brig Young Gregory, at Havana, six days from Sisal, we have received advice from Merida, the Capital of Yucatan, which reach to the 10th ultimo. We translate as follows. The old Legislature (Assembly) has been dissolved, and a new and extraordinary Congress was in session. It was opened with the greatest solemnity, by Miguel Barbachano, who was appointed Governor interim, by the assembly, and has since been elected Governor of Yucatan, by the Congress. The names of the other Government officers are also given. The first operation of the new Congress was to settle the question of Independence. This being done, they proceeded to the management and regulation of all the other matters necessary to the establishment of a new Government. Three persons have been appointed on a secret foreign mission, via the United States! Although the Government did not openly declare that these officers were to visit Washington for the purpose of enquiring into the steps necessary to procure annexation, yet this was well known to be the object. This step has found great favor with the people, and although the mission was via the United States to some other country, yet it was well understood.

The Navy.

List of Officers attached to the United States Ship Dale, bound to the Pacific Ocean:—*Commander,* Wm. W. McKean. *Lieutenants,* Edward M. Yard, T. A. M. Craven, Fabius Stanly, Wm. Taylor Smith. *Acting Master,* Nath'l. C. Bryant. *Surgeon,* Daniel S. Green. *Ass't. Surgeon,* John Rudenstein. *Purser,* McKean Buchanan. *P. Mid'n.* J. Downs, Jr., John Febiger, J. B. Creighton. *Mids,* Allen T. Byrons. *Act. Mids,* Wm. B. Hayes, Thomas B. Houston, John Adams. J. R. Hamilton.

Courtesy Bancroft Library, University of California, Berkeley.

The first edition of The California Star, San Francisco's first newspaper.

Numerous Irish politicians have served both the state and country. Although seldom thought of any longer as a distinct and separate group, Irish influence has remained strong. The sons and daughters of Eire continue to charm, even in California's pluralistic society.

Sam Brannan

Sam Brannan's story combines many of the possible triumphs and excesses common in Gold Rush California. His father came to America from Ireland in 1775 and located in Maine. Sam was born in 1812, the fifth child of his father's second marriage.

When a young man Brannan was baptised as a Mormon by his friend, William Smith, one of the founders of the Mormon Church. Sam had learned the printer's trade and was enterprising and adventuresome. Though not much of a religious zealot, he agreed to lead a group of church members to California, where a new colony was to be formed. In 1846, after a voyage around Cape Horn, with a stop in the Hawaiian Islands, Sam Brannan landed with 300 Mormons at Yerba Buena. The group included merchants, tradesmen, physicians, and lawyers plus 65 women and 40 children. They tripled the population of their new home town.

The American Navy already occupied the port, but the war with Mexico was still unsettled. Brannan quickly established a number of firsts in the emerging town. A disgruntled passenger accused him of embezzling part of the fare money. He stood trial and was found innocent by the first jury trial in San Francisco. In 1847, he founded the first newspaper, the California Star. He published San Francisco's first book and, as a church elder, preached its first sermon and performed the first marriage. He also helped promote the first public school.

The Gold Rush found Brannan not a miner but a merchant. He established general stores in San Francisco and the Sacramento Valley and became a millionaire. The Mormons expelled him from the church in 1848, when he claimed, with apparent honesty, that his bookkeeping system could not account for all the money he had spent on church related affairs. The Mormons dispersed. Brigham Young, despite Sam's urging to settle in California, decided to make the Mormon headquarters in Utah.

No matter, Brannan continued as a civic leader and member of the San Francisco City Council. He bought downtown lots and was a leader of the Vigilante Committees of 1851 and 1856, which helped purge the city of criminals. His income swelled to an enormous amount, $250,000 to $500,000 a year.

His fortunes began to slide as he drank more champagne and invited everyone in sight to join him. His second marriage began to unravel. His wife and children moved to Switzerland. Sam's interest shifted to the Napa Valley, where he bought 2,000 acres of valley land and 800 acres of hill property. He planted grapes, built a brandy distillery, and supported the growing wine industry. An elaborate hotel was built in Calistoga. He touted the local geysers and mineral baths as a health spa. There was a costly divorce, then his empire almost disappeared in various economic misfortunes.

A final, if modest, reprieve came in the early 1880's. Brannan remembered that 20 years earlier he had bought bonds issued by the forces of Benito Juarez, then fighting the forces of French-sponsored Emperor Maximilian for control of Mexico. Brannan had even spent $30,000 to sponsor an army of unemployed American Civil War veterans to help Juarez. Everyone thought the bonds would be worthless, but Juarez had won, and the Mexicans remembered Brannan's help. After years of negotiation they finally settled the debt for $49,000.

Brannan had taken a third wife in Mexico during his days there, but she decided not to return with him to California. He died in Escondido in 1889, where he was enthusiastically trying to sell local real estate. He was a good man, generous and creative, but marred by alcoholism.

CHAPTER 17
AFRICAN AMERICANS WERE AMONG THE EARLIEST CALIFORNIA SETTLERS
James P. Beckwourth, William A. Leidesdorff,
Mammy (Mary Ellen) Pleasant
Jackie (Jack Roosevelt) Robinson, Alice Walker

A MAN OF AFRICAN DESCENT, Pedro Alonzo Nino, sailed with Christopher Columbus on his first voyage to the New World. Other blacks and mulattoes were with the earliest Spanish explorers. Many Africans had migrated to Spain during the long rule of the Moors. Having become integrated into Spanish life, it was natural they and their descendants would have a part in the new ventures.

In New Spain the cruel policies of the Spaniards soon exterminated most of the local Indians. An acute labor shortage developed, a condition that was solved by importing slaves from Africa. The first royal decree permitting transportation of slaves was signed in 1501. To encourage Spanish migration to New Spain, each immigrant was allowed to take as many as twelve slaves. By 1527 about 10,000 slaves from Africa had arrived.

No one knows how many Africans were captured and sent off to the Spanish colonies. Some estimates are over 15,000,000 slaves. They accompanied Cortes in his battles to conquer Mexico, and almost certainly went on the earliest voyages to California. Many were rebellious, some escaped, disease and hardship claimed others. However, an inexhaustible supply of replacements were provided by the African slave traders.

During the days of the missions and Mexican rule in California, persons of pure and mixed African blood were a significant part of the population. 18% of the population of Alta California is estimated to have been black in 1790 . Francisco Reyes, an African American, owned the San Fernando Valley and became Mayor of Los Angeles during the

1790's. Another African, known as Bob, with his white shipmate, Thomas Dark, deserted their ship from Boston in California in 1816. They became the first American residents of Alta California. Bob became Juan Cristobal, married a Mexican and became a prosperous landowner. Four men of African American inheritance were governors of Mexican California between 1837 and 1847.

The Gold Rush of 1849 and statehood in 1850 had profound effects on the status of African Americans in California. They came to pan gold, but there were relatively few of them. The 1850 California Census lists only 962 black people. During the Gold Rush they were never more than 1% of the population.

Like all non-whites, African Americans experienced much rejection and a variety of legal discriminations. Whites tried to deny black ownership of claims in the gold fields. The first state legislature banned blacks from voting or serving in the militia. They could not testify against a white man in court. Their children could not attend white schools. An 1860 law allowed only people of Caucasian descent to file for homesteads.

California came into the Union in 1850 as a "free" or non-slave state, so slavery was not supposed to exist. In many states, of course, it was legal. Southern slave holders brought their slaves to California, hoping to have an advantage by their use in digging out the gold. There was a sharp clash in attitudes amongst whites about this. Some blacks escaped from slave states, hoping to find gold in California, and, if necessary, buy their freedom.

A federal law passed in 1850 gave slave owners the right to recapture and reclaim runaway slaves. Most California courts upheld this law, which set a time when the owner needed to have the slave out of the state. These orders were often ignored. Some slave owners even taunted the anti-slavery public by advertising their slaves for sale to anyone wishing to set them free. Not uncommonly this was done. The slave owner was happy to avoid the cost and trouble of taking his property back to a slave state.

Civil injustices to African Americans brought protests from their community. State conventions of the Convention of Colored Citizens of California were held in 1855, 1856, 1857, and 1865 to protest the inability of blacks to vote, acquire homesteads, and testify in court against whites. These meetings had no obvious immediate effect. In 1857 a bill was introduced in the state legislature which would have excluded any-

Frederick Remington sketch of a post-Civil War cavalryman. Blacks have served with military distinction throughout our history.

one of African descent from California, the supreme insult and threat to civil rights.

More favorable places to live were investigated. New Granada (present day Columbia and Panama) and Vancouver Island in Canada seemed promising. Perhaps 800 black people did move to Vancouver Island. The exclusionary bill failed to pass the legislature, and these questions were soon superseded by the Civil War.

California had little involvment in the Civil War. As a free state California sided with the North, and its gold provided important backing for the Union cause. Few Californians, white or black, took part in the fighting. Persons of African descent were excluded by law from military service, but a few did join the northern armies. At home they served in the Home Guards.

The Emancipation Proclamation of 1863 freed the slaves. The Thirteenth Amendment to the U.S. Constitution formally outlawed slavery in 1865. Voting rights for African Americans became a reality with the Fifteenth Amendment passed in 1869. An 1863 law gave them the right to testify in court. However, segregated schools in California were legalized in 1870.

James P. Beckwourth

James P. Beckwourth was a legendary frontier African American. He was born in 1798 of black and white parentage. He was apprenticed to a St. Louis blacksmith for five years but never liked the trade. At age 19 Beckwourth decided to go West, and he became a trapper with Colonel Ashley's Rocky Mountain Fur Company.

Beckwourth also became a member of the Crow Indian tribe when an elderly squaw thought he was a long lost son. He took the name "Morning Star" and attained the rank of chief. He became famous for his bravery while fighting enemies of the Crows.

Always restless, Beckwourth wandered the West. In 1843 he became a prominent American supporter of the effort to free California from Mexico. In 1850 he discovered the mountain pass northwest of Reno named in his honor. Like many men of his age, civilization appealed little to him. Myth says he was poisoned by the Crows at a feast,when he refused to rejoin the tribe. But he probably died alone of food poisoning on his way to a Crow village.

James P. Beckwourth, explorer and scout.

The City Hotel, owned by William Leidesdorff, was San Francisco's first hotel.

Courtesy Bancroft Library, University of California, Berkeley.

William Leidesdorff, early San Francisco businessman and civic leader.

Courtesy Bancroft Library, University of California, Berkeley.

William A. Leidesdorff

William A. Leidesdorff was a West Indian who came to San Francisco in his own 106 ton schooner at the age of 21. His father was white and his mother black. From 1841 to1845 he operated a trading vessel to

*Mammy (Mary Ellen) Pleasant,
pre-Civil War San Francisco
businesswoman and
civil rights leader.*

Courtesy Bancroft Library.

Hawaii, when Thomas Larkin appointed him American vice-consul in San Francisco. In 1846 he bought several pieces of property in what is now the financial district and in 1847 built San Francisco's first hotel. He also piloted the first steamship into San Francisco Bay.

Leidesdorff served on San Francisco's first school board and helped supervise the building of the city's first public school. He became the growing town's first treasurer. The Mexican government gave him a land grant of 35,000 acres near Sutter's Fort, and in addition he owned a vast tract of land where the city of Lafayette is now located. Leidesdorff died at age 38 in 1848.

Mammy (Mary Ellen) Pleasant

Mammy (Mary Ellen) Pleasant was the most influential African American woman of Gold Rush California. She was born a slave in Georgia in 1814. Her father was Hawaiian and her mother was African. Unusually intelligent, she was sent to be educated in Boston, where she became acquainted with many white abolitionists. She married a wealthy African American businessman, Alexander Smith, inherited considerable money upon his death, and moved to San Francisco in 1849 with her second husband, John Pleasant. There she opened a res-

146

*Jackie Robinson
in Dodger uniform.
He played first base,
second base and outfield
for the Dodgers.*

Courtesy Los Angeles Dodgers, Inc.

taurant and invested in real estate. Her keen intelligence was respected by the entire community. She helped many anti-slavery causes and allegedly gave John Brown $30,000 to help finance his slave rebellion in Virginia in 1858. She also supported the Convention of Colored People in California and aided many runaway slaves.

Following the Civil War, there was a gradual increase in the black Californian population. By 1940 the state's black population was 124,306. More than half of these people lived in the Los Angeles area. Immigration of African Americans to California accelerated sharply as a result of World War II. Between 1940 and 1950 the black population in California increased 272% to 462,172. The main attractions were jobs in the state's booming steel mills, shipyards, and aircraft industries. In 1941 the federal government decreed that defense industries must prevent racial discrimination in hiring, which undercut long established union exclusion of black people from jobs. Prejudice against African Americans, though lessening, is still a blight in job hiring in California.

Discrimination against black citizens in military service continued into World War II. Only near the war's end in 1945 was a plan proposed to integrate fighting units. Some 700,000 blacks served in the Army, 165,000 in the Navy, 5,000 in the Coast Guard, and 17,000 in the Marines. Over 600 were trained and served in the Air Force. During the

Korean and Viet Nam wars black servicemen served and were killed at rates much higher than their proportion in the population.

Jackie (Jack Roosevelt) Robinson

Georgia-born Jackie Robinson grew up in Pasadena and became a star athlete at the University of California at Los Angeles. He pioneered the full acceptance of African Americans into professional sports when he was signed to play with the Brooklyn Dodgers baseball team in 1945. Robinson played second base with the Dodger's farm club at Montreal in 1946 and led the International League in batting. In 1947 he was brought up to Brooklyn, the first black athlete in major league baseball. Quickly he became a superstar. Since then black athletes have been outstanding performers in professional and college teams.

After his athletic career, Robinson was an active worker in civil rights affairs.

Roughly paralleling the emergence of black athletes has been the rise of African Americans in music and all entertainment. The performers are legion and well beloved to all sections of the American public. They have given us our uniquely American art form, jazz.

Alice Walker

Alice Walker is an African American who became nationally prominent with the publication of her novel, The Color Purple. She received the American Book Award and the Pulitzer Prize for the book in 1983. It was made into a very successful movie in 1985.

One of eight children, Ms. Walker was born into a family of sharecroppers in Georgia. She attended Spelman College in Georgia, then Sarah Lawrence College in New York, where she received a B.A. degree in 1965. After college she lived for several years in Mississippi as a civil rights worker. As her writing became more successful, recognition came to her as a poet, essayist, and writer of short stories and novels. Also, she became a visiting professor in literature at several universities. Her research interests have focused on feminist writers, especially black women authors. Literary efforts have been combined with active participation in many political causes having to do with human rights, nuclear disarmament, and feminism.

Alice Walker, writer and intellectual.

Her writings have called for recognition of the rights, worth, and dignity of black women. This is combined with a plea to African Americans to maintain their individuality and uniqueness. A sustaining and curative love between two black sisters is the central theme of The Color Purple. Walker's consistent emphasis is feminist. One of her goals is to publicize neglected black women writers of the past.

She now lives in northern California, is publisher of Wild Trees Press, and continues to devote most of her time to writing and lecturing. She has a college-age daughter.

Several African Americans have reached the top in California politics. Augustus F. Hawkins was the first black person elected to the U. S. House of Representatives in 1962. Thomas Bradley was elected mayor of California's largest city, Los Angeles, in 1973. Wilson Riles was the first to win a state office, State Superintendent of Public Instruction, in 1970. Willie L. Brown, Jr. became majority leader of the California Legislative Assembly in 1980. Many other black people have won high office at both the national and local levels.

*Tom Bradley,
long-term Los Angeles
mayor.*

In 1988 California's black population was 2.09 million, 7.5% of the population. But the many economic and social troubles of the black community continue to be severe. Correcting the problems has been a long time coming. Full participation in the state's bounty still remains a goal for most black Americans.

CHAPTER 18
THE CHINESE COME TO THE "GOLDEN MOUNTAINS"
Choh Hao Li, Yuan T. Lee

BEFORE THE GOLD STRIKE AT SUTTER'S MILL, only a few dozen Chinese had come to California. But with the crackling expectancy of riches to be made Chinese soon heard the call of the "Golden Mountains." Those were hard times in China. The Qing dynasty had been in power for hundreds of years but was becoming more ineffective and harsh. Immigration from China was a crime punishable by beheading, but most young men had little fear of being caught.

Over 90% of the adventuresome Chinese who left for California were single men. They were mostly farmers or fishermen, from the province of Guangdong, a small area in south China near Hong Kong, about the size of the San Francisco Bay Area. Only in recent decades have sizeable numbers of Chinese come to America from the northern provinces and from the professional and merchant classes.

Perhaps half the voyagers saw themselves as visitors rather than settlers. A great many did return to China because of hardships found in the Golden State. The Chinese settlements in California had a strong bachelor quality because Chinese women had legally been excluded. In 1880 20 times as many Chinese men were in the U. S. as there were Chinese women.

The sea passage cost about $100. Many simply paid their own way or borrowed from Chinese sources. When the Chinese became a favored source of labor, American companies contracted with Chinese brokers to find workers, and the passage money was deducted from future earnings. Abuse of the system in the United States was controlled by law after California entered the Union in 1850 as a "free" state.

Bad as conditions were in California for Chinese immigrants, they were worse in Cuba and South America. Many Chinese were actually kidnapped in China and sent off to Latin America as near slaves, despite an international ban of the slave trade in 1862.

Upon arriving in the U. S., usually in San Francisco, Orientals found a less than cordial reception. Because of their language, skin color, long braided hair, and strange clothing, the Chinese were conspicuous. Only 325 came in 1849; 450 in 1850. Afterwards much larger numbers arrived, until the Exclusion Act of 1882.

The men set off for the mines. After the first few years, mining had become frustrating. Gold nuggets could no longer be picked up in every stream. Mining required muscle-wrenching work with pick and shovel. About a third of the miners came from Southern states, with strong prejudices against non-whites. Many white miners didn't do well and resented the methodical, uncomplaining Chinese, who lived cheaply and saved their money. There began to emerge a series of State and Federal laws to curb the Chinese. These restrictions became popular political issues for both the Republican and Democratic Parties. That the spirit of the regulations was opposed to the struggle for equal rights central in the Civil War was scarcely raised as an argument. The rhetoric of the day was that California and the whole country was awash with "hordes" of Chinese who worked cheaper than whites and ruined the economy for everyone.

Actually the Chinese never were numerous in the country or even in California. In the first 33 years of migration 300,000 entered the U. S. and two-thirds returned to China. The Chinese were about 10% of California's population.

But strong measures were taken to control them. In 1854 a California law forbade Chinese from testifying in court against whites. Indians and Blacks were forbidden also. In 1850 a special Foreign Miner's Tax of $3 to $20 a month was devised as an attempt to drive the Chinese from the gold mines. This tax was difficult to collect, but at one time it raised half of the State's revenue. In 1860 a special tax was placed on Chinese fishermen. In1870 a law forbade Chinese to own land in California. Chinese women could not enter California without special certificates. In 1885 state law prohibited Chinese children from attending public schools. The labor union movement, which developed in the 1880's, wanted no Chinese participation.

Despite everything, the Chinese immigrants survived and made significant contributions to the State's development. It would be stretching a point to say they prospered. They worked in the gold mines and a few

Chinese at work mining for gold.

Chinese were important in building the transcontinental railroad.

became rich. Many even made the transition to heavily mechanized hydraulic mining. In 1867 40% to 50% still worked in the mines.

Their greatest early fame came as laborers on the transcontinental railroad, which was completed in 1869. The railroad was built by two crews working toward Promontory, Utah, where they met and drove in a last ceremonial golden spike. The work party coming from the west started in Sacramento and carved its way through and over the Sierra Nevada mountains. It was the greatest construction project of the 19th century. Charles Crocker was in charge of the western construction. Cornish miners from England were first used, but it was difficult to keep white workers; they quit to go off to the gold mines or the newly discovered silver mines in Nevada. Crocker saw the Chinese as a solution. At one time there were 15,000 Chinese working for him as "Crocker's pets".

This is how Crocker described them: "They proved nearly equal to white men in the amount of labor they perform, and are much more reliable. No danger of strikes among them. We are training them to all kinds of labor: blasting, driving horses, handling rock as well as pick and shovel."

The Chinese workers earned $28.00 a month and provided their own food and shelter. At times they were blasting and hauling rock on ledges and tunnels as high as 2,000 feet above the American River. They worked through summer heat and deep winter snow. The final result was a great success. The Big Four financiers, Leland Stanford, C.P. Huntington, Mark Hopkins, and Charles Crocker became wealthy. The Chinese looked for other things to do.

California was becoming an agricultural state. For a time wheat was the major crop. Grapes and wine making became established. The Chinese provided much of the farm labor. They were also pioneers in developing fisheries. They spread out into small towns throughout the State.

The 1870's brought a severe persistent recession in California. Unemployment reached 30%. Bank failures wiped out savings. The Chinese became the agreed-on scapegoat. Denis Kearney formed the Workingmen's Party and became the spokesman for these rascist sentiments. In 1882 the final crushing blow came when anti-Chinese prejudice was legalized when Congress passed the Chinese Exclusion Act. This prohibited immigration of Chinese laborers into the U.S. for ten years and prohibited them from becoming naturalized citizens. Native born children

154

Courtesy Bancroft Library, University of California, Berkeley.

A drawing of the Chinese quarter in San Francisco in 1873.

Two Chinese ladies in San Francisco in the 1880s.

had been guaranteed citizenship since 1868 when the 14th Amendment was passed. Chinese wives could not enter the country. Teachers, students, merchants, tourists, and diplomats could visit from China only under supervision. Provisions of the law were extended by subsequent laws, until the Magnuson Act repealed these restrictions in 1943.

The effect was ravaging. The Chinese were driven out of their small footholds in smaller towns around the state. Many went back to China. The larger Chinatowns developed a seige mentality. The power and prestige of the large commercial and benevolent Six Companies diminished. Tongs, gangs organized to protect vice activities, became active around 1875. Prostitution and gambling flourished. There were few Chinese women and many were girls kidnapped in China and forced into prostitution. Opium smoking became common. In 1900 the U.S. Chinese population was only about 90,000.

Small adjustments were still possible. In the Gold Rush days getting laundry done was difficult in an almost all male society. Some men actually sent their shirts to Hong Kong, to be washed and ironed at a cost of $12.00 a dozen. By 1870 there were 2,000 Chinese laundries in San Francisco. After the Exclusion Act it was safer to be a laundryman-merchant than a laborer, a classification that gave some protection against deportation. In 1920 about 30% of all Chinese were in laundry work.

The 1906 earthquake destroyed many immigration records. A Chinese could visit China and upon his return tell the Immigration Service he had a son while there. This created a "slot" for a Chinese young man to enter the U.S. These attempted entries were subject to intense scrutiny at Angel Island in San Francisco Bay, which opened in 1910. Interrogations lasted for days, and some immigrants were kept on the island as long as two years. Only one person in four was admitted.

World War II brought an upturn in Chinese fortunes. Their young men served in the U.S. armed forces, and China was a valued ally. Most Chinese residents were already citizens, because they had been born in this country. The restrictive laws were recognized as incompatible with national ideals. Angel Island closed in 1940 and prospective immigrants were screened at their country of origin. The Chinese Exclusion Act was repealed. In 1945 the War Brides Act allowed Chinese wives of servicemen into the Country.

Entry of Chinese immigrants has finally been liberalized. In 1955 170,000 immigrants a year were allowed from the Eastern Hemisphere with a 20,000 limit from each country. In 1978 this was changed to allow 270,000 into the U.S. from the whole world. A very high percentage of the new Chinese immigrants have been women.

The end of the Vietnam War in 1975 brought a determined effort by the North Vietnamese to rid the country of the over 1 million Chinese who lived there. Like the Jews in Europe during World War II, they became subject to persecution and extortion. As much as $5,000 a person was demanded for permission to leave the country. Most of the "Boat People" who fled Vietnam were ethnic Chinese. Large numbers of these refugees found their way eventually to California.

Choh Hao Li

The ability to simplify the complicated found expression in the life of Dr. Choh Hao Li. The great biochemist was born in Canton, China, in 1913, one of eleven children. Dr. Li graduated from the University of Nanking in 1933, then stayed on to teach there for two years. Then he

Choh Hao Li, Ph.D.; Eminent endocrinologist holds a molecular model of a human pituitary hormone.

Yuan T. Lee, Ph.D., Professor of Chemistry and 1986 Nobel Prize winner.

decided to come to the United States for an advanced degree in chemistry. A brother was a student at the University of California at Berkeley. Choh Hao, who had already published a scientific paper in English, convinced the head of the department to take him as a probationary student for a semester. He went on to get a Ph.D. at Berkeley in 1938. A professional lifetime was spent at the University unraveling the chemistry and biology of the pituitary gland.

A cubicle in the basement became the starting point of a career that led to a professorship, director of the Hormone Research Laboratory at the University of California Medical Center in San Francisco, and the systematic clarification of the puzzle of the tiny but powerful adenohypophysis of the pituitary gland. Using thousands of pulverized animal glands, he and his co-workers were able to synthesize a protein useful in treating children stunted by a shortage of the hormone. Other hormones produced by the gland which affect fat metabolism, milk production, sexual development, and the regulation of other vital processes have been isolated and identified in his laboratory.

The Chinese immigrant spoke on his philosophy on receiving an award for his achievements in 1979. He titled the speech FATE AND FAITH: MY PERSONAL EXPERIENCES. In Chinese and Buddhist thought, these forces compete in every person's life. Fate is what you were born with, what you were meant to be. However, Faith creates self-confidence and belief in the possibility of ultimate success through the use of what comes your way. Dr. Li felt that his life showed both truths at work.

The esteemed professor is now retired. He became a U.S. citizen in 1955, has three children, and lives with his wife in Berkeley.

Yuan T. Lee

This professor of chemistry at the University of California, Berkeley, became the fifteenth winner of the Nobel Prize from the university faculty. His award in 1986 gave the California immigrant from the Republic of China the world's highest award in science.

Yuan T. Lee was born in Hsinchu, Taiwan, in 1936. His father is a professor of art at the University of Taiwan and one of that country's most famous painters. In his youth Yuan was deterred from becoming a painter by his father, who felt discouraged by the economic prospects of a young person starting an art career. He recalls that a high point of his early school career was playing on the championship Taiwan grade school table tennis team. Reading a biography of the great Polish-French chemist, Madame Marie Curie, inspired his interest in science. Marie Curie with her husband discovered the elements Polonium and Radium and won two Nobel Prizes.

Dr. Lee came to the United States for his postgraduate education in chemistry and received a Ph.D. from the University of California, Berkeley, in 1965. In 1974 he became a professor at Berkeley and a U.S. citizen. His award, shared with two other chemists, came for describing the exact manner in which chemical reactions take place.

A modest man, Dr. Lee admits that often he cannot explain scientific reactions outside his field of study. He lives with his wife and three children in Berkeley.

The Chinese characteristics of intelligence, respect for moral values, capacity for hard work at any task, and devotion to education are continuing their contribution to American life. Chinese-Americans may have found the "Golden Mountains" in California after all.

CHAPTER 19
THE JAPANESE IN CALIFORNIA
Manjiro Nakahama

IT ALL BEGAN WITH A HAPPY ADVENTURE. The first Japanese immigrant to America or California was a 14 year old shipwrecked fisherman, Manjiro Nakahama.

In 1841 he was marooned for several months with four other crewmen on an unhabited island off Japan. They were rescued by Captain William H. Whitfield, whose New Bedford whaling ship, John Howland, was returning to Massachusetts. American ships were not allowed to make port in Japan, so the men had to go with the Americans. When they reached Hawaii, Manjiro's shipmates decided to stay there and try to find a way home. Captain Whitfield and Manjiro had become good friends, and the Japanese decided to stay with the ship.

In New Bedford the captain found him a home with friends. Manjiro became a student and excelled in mathematics and navigation. In 1846 he went back to sea. After a three year whaling voyage he tried his hand at mining gold in California. There were no Japanese in California, as it was illegal for them to leave the home country. Manjiro did find gold, which he exchanged for 600 pieces of silver.

Manjiro had a plan to get back to Japan. He bought a whaleboat in Hawaii and named it *Adventure*. Then he arranged for an American whaler to transport himself, two Japanese shipmates and the whaleboat to home waters. They were put over the side four miles off Okinawa. His boat was loaded with books, gifts, and other American purchases. Okinawa was Japanese, but Manjiro could not understand the local dialect. He was kept in custody for a year and a half for intensive questioning about his experiences, then allowed to visit his widowed mother in Japan.

Manjiro Nakahama at about age 40.

Courtesy Hiroshi Nakahama.

Manjiro became a respected national resource. It was 1853-54, and Japan was about to be visited by Commodore Perry and several U.S. Navy ships. The ruling shoguns had closed Japan to foreigners in the early 1600's, except for the Dutch, who were allowed to visit a tiny island in Nagasaki harbor. Japanese had been forbidden to leave the country since 1636. The authorities had a million questions about the customs and etiquette to be followed during Perry's visit. There were even enquiries such as, "How is it possible for American's to live without rice?"

Manjiro instructed the Japanese authorities in English, which they much valued, but the shogun's advisors advised against allowing him to have direct contacts with Americans as an adviser; they were afraid that his appreciation for past American kindnesses might make him less than objective. Also he was considered lower class, being from a fisherman's family. During Perry's visit the Japanese authorities listened to Manjiro's counsel that trade and communication should be opened with the United States. His descriptions of American technology convinced the

162

Japanese that much of value could be learned. He was given a position as an instructor at a newly established naval training school and translated an English language text on navigation and engineering into Japanese.

The Japanese reciprocated Commodore Perry's visits by sending 100 Japanese to Washington, D.C., in 1860 for the ratification of a treaty of friendship and trade between the two countries. The Japanese officials were received by President Buchanan. Manjiiro Nakahama went along as a navigator in the escort ship for the official party. Again he was rejected as an official interpreter by the Japanese government. His ship stopped in San Francisco, where he astonished a shopkeeper by asking to buy a Webster's Dictionary in perfect English. He also took back to Japan sewing machines, cameras, and other inventions not available in his homeland. In 1870 he accompanied another Japanese visit to the United States and Europe. He died in 1898. This remarkable person is remembered as a great teacher and promoter of Japanese-American friendship.

Immigration to America by Japanese had to wait for political change at home. The clan of Tokugawa had ruled the country since 1600. The emperor had been pushed into the background and stripped of power. In 1868 the Tokugawas were ousted and the emperor regained control. Economic conditions were bad in Japan. Also, many people wished to avoid military conscription. However, most immigrants to America remained attached to their home country and considered returning if their economic fortunes improved.

In 1868 a few Japanese came to California under contract as agricultural workers. In 1869 a group of now unemployed warriors (samurai) and tradesmen tried to start a farming colony near Placerville, California, at Gold Hill, called the Wakamatsu Tea and Silk Farm Colony. Some 50,000 mulberry trees, bamboo shoots, tea seeds, and other plants were planted on 600 acres. The experiment failed after two years, apparently because of the different climate and soil conditions.

The trickle of immigrants gradually increased. In 1886 only 194 came. In 1898 there were 2,230. By 1890 there were 107,000 Chinese and 2,039 Japanese in California. In 1940 there were 77,504 Chinese and 126,947 Japanese in California.

Like the Chinese they were sought by industries looking for cheap, reliable labor. After the available supply of Chinese labor decreased because of discouragement and many returned home, Japanese replaced them. A brisk business developed in finding workers in Japan and arranging passports and passage. About half worked in some kind of agricultural job. Few Californians wanted the Japanese to stay, and although they were not forced to go back to Japan after completing their jobs, laws were passed requiring proof they had the funds to return.

Most of the immigrants were men. These were the first generation, the Issei.

The Japanese soon met with the same prejudices heaped on the Chinese. Everyone agreed that they were intelligent and marvelous workers, but feared, that if given any chance, they would soon own the State. The cry was that white men could not compete with them. The Japanese worked too hard, were willing to take less pay, and got ahead by working their wives and children. They saved their money and bought land. Somehow they made poor land bear crops. There was always the suspician that their loyalty was to their homeland. In general, they were strange and different, not persons to assimilate in America's melting pot.

Several national and state laws were passed to thwart the Issei. Japanese were denied citizenship on the ground that naturalization was permitted only to "free white persons and to aliens of African nativity and persons of African descent." After the Civil War in 1870 blacks were allowed to become citizens. The Japanese, neither white nor black, didn't qualify. This interpretation was upheld by the U.S. Supreme Court in 1922.

In 1908 the federal government negotiated a "Gentlemen's Agreement" with Japan, whereby no more skilled or unskilled laborers were allowed to emigrate to the U.S. In 1913 California passed a law prohibiting land ownership by aliens ineligible for citizenship. This was widely evaded by putting land ownership in the name of children. In 1924 a new Immigration Act totally excluded "all immigrants ineligible to citizenship". The door had been barred to the Issei. Their children born in America, however, automatically became citizens.

World War II brought the situation into an even more painful state. The attack on Pearl Harbor on December 7, 1941, made many Americans feel that Japanese-Americans must in some way have been collaborators. There were stories of Japanese planes being guided by arrows cut in sugar cane fields, secret radio messages, etc. The nation was outraged and frightened.

WESTERN DEFENSE COMMAND AND FOURTH ARMY
WARTIME CIVIL CONTROL ADMINISTRATION
Presidio of San Francisco, California
May 3, 1942

INSTRUCTIONS
TO ALL PERSONS OF
JAPANESE
ANCESTRY
Living in the Following Area:

All of the County of San Mateo, State of California.

Pursuant to the provisions of Civilian Exclusion Order No. 35, this Headquarters, dated May 3, 1942, all persons of Japanese ancestry, both alien and non-alien, will be evacuated from the above area by 12 o'clock noon, P. W. T., Saturday, May 9, 1942.

No Japanese person living in the above area will be permitted to change residence after 12 o'clock noon, P. W. T., Sunday, May 3, 1942, without obtaining special permission from the representative of the Commanding General, Northern California Sector, at the Civil Control Station located at:

Masonic Temple Building,
100 North Ellsworth Street,
San Mateo, California.

Such permits will only be granted for the purpose of uniting members of a family, or in cases of grave emergency.

The Civil Control Station is equipped to assist the Japanese population affected by this evacuation in the following ways:

1. Give advice and instructions on the evacuation.
2. Provide services with respect to the management, leasing, sale, storage or other disposition of most kinds of property, such as real estate, business and professional equipment, household goods, boats, automobiles and livestock.
3. Provide temporary residence elsewhere for all Japanese in family groups.
4. Transport persons and a limited amount of clothing and equipment to their new residence.

The Following Instructions Must Be Observed:

1. A responsible member of each family, preferably the head of the family, or the person in whose name most of the property is held, and each individual living alone, will report to the Civil Control Station to receive further instructions. This must be done between 8:00 A. M. and 5:00 P. M. on Monday, May 4, 1942, or between 8:00 A. M. and 5:00 P. M. on Tuesday, May 5, 1942.
2. Evacuees must carry with them on departure for the Assembly Center, the following property:
  (a) Bedding and linens (no mattress) for each member of the family;
  (b) Toilet articles for each member of the family;
  (c) Extra clothing for each member of the family;
  (d) Sufficient knives, forks, spoons, plates, bowls and cups for each member of the family;
  (e) Essential personal effects for each member of the family.

All items carried will be securely packaged, tied and plainly marked with the name of the owner and numbered in accordance with instructions obtained at the Civil Control Station. The size and number of packages is limited to that which can be carried by the individual or family group.

3. No pets of any kind will be permitted.
4. No personal items and no household goods will be shipped to the Assembly Center.
5. The United States Government through its agencies will provide for the storage, at the sole risk of the owner, of the more substantial household items, such as iceboxes, washing machines, pianos and other heavy furniture. Cooking utensils and other small items will be accepted for storage if crated, packed and plainly marked with the name and address of the owner. Only one name and address will be used by a given family.
6. Each family, and individual living alone, will be furnished transportation to the Assembly Center or will be authorized to travel by private automobile in a supervised group. All instructions pertaining to the movement will be obtained at the Civil Control Station.

Go to the Civil Control Station between the hours of 8:00 A. M. and 5:00 P. M., Monday, May 4, 1942, or between the hours of 8:00 A. M. and 5:00 P. M., Tuesday, May 5, 1942, to receive further instructions.

J. L. DeWITT
Lieutenant General, U. S. Army
Commanding

SEE CIVILIAN EXCLUSION ORDER NO. 35.

Courtesy Bancroft Library, University of California, Berkeley.

1942 notice of evacuation and internment of California Japanese-American citizens.

An attack on the West Coast was considered a distinct possibility. Actually there were only three ineffective attacks by the Japanese navy. A submarine fired a couple of shells at the coast near Santa Barbara, another submarine shot at shore batteries near Astoria, Oregon, and a plane tried to set a forest fire in Oregon with incendiary bombs. There was no evidence that Japanese Americans were guilty of disloyalty. Even so, the military, many politicians, and a lot of the public felt the Japanese were a danger to the country.

The 1940 census listed 126,947 persons of Japanese ancestry living in the continental United States. Almost all lived in the three western states. There were 40,869 aliens denied citizenship (Issei) and 71,484 citizens by birth (Nisei). Several thousand Nisei were already in the armed forces. They were declared aliens, not subject to military duty, and discharged. After pondering the problem the federal government decided that all Japanese were to be evacuated from the western half of California, Oregon, and Washington, and the southern third of Arizona. This became law on February 19, 1942, despite no evidence of disloyalty by a Japanese-American. The absence of proof was considered an indication of impending danger, that the Japanese had clever plans which would be unleashed at the appropriate time.

Ten detention camps, located in California, Idaho, Wyoming, Colorado, Utah, Arizona, and Arkansas, were built outside the forbidden areas, and administered by the federal War Relocation Agency. The camps were built from scratch in barren, uninhabited areas, and 107,000 men, women, and children moved in after November 1, 1942. Prior to that the evacuees had been detained in racetrack stables, fairgounds, and other unused facilities near their homes.

When the clamor for incarceration died down, calmer heads began to have influence. After a year detainees who passed security checks were allowed to leave the camps to live and work outside. The Army recruited many Nisei to use as translators and intelligence specialists. The Nisei pressed for permission to serve in the Army in a combat role to demonstrate their loyalty. In January, 1943, plans were made to form the 442nd Regimental Combat Team. This unit, together with the Nisei 100th Regiment, fought with great valor and inflicted heavy casualties against the Germans in Italy and France. Some 33,000 Nisei served in World War II.

In January, 1945, the U.S. Supreme Court ruled that the evacuation order creating the camps, right or wrong, had been properly made as an

*Two Japanese-
American ladies
work in the farm
of an internment
camp.*

Courtesy Bancroft Library, University of California, Berkeley.

Courtesy Bancroft Library, University of California, Berkeley.

*A typical
relocation
camp building.*

Japanese-American kids in a relocation camp have some fun despite the unpleasant circumstances.

Courtesy Bancroft Library, University of California, Berkeley.

act of national defense, but that loyal Nisei could not be prevented by the government from returning to their homes.

After World War II past legal restraints against Japanese-Americans were abolished. The Walter-McCarran Immigration Act of 1952 repealed the old law banning Japanese immigration. California revoked the law forbidding ownership of property. The federal government paid out $38,000,000 in claims for financial loss caused by detention, but this was only about ten percent of the actual losses.

An ironic twist in this story occurred in Hawaii, where about 160,000 people were Japanese, a third of the population. There was talk of relocating them to California camps, but the difficulties were so great that only 1,875 were detained because of suspected disloyalty.

As a token of redress, Congress in 1988 voted to give to each living Japanese-American internee of World War II $20,000 and an official apology from the U. S. government. It was a small payment for the old wrong.

The history of racial prejudice, unfair restrictions, and bigotry against Japanese-Americans should sadden us all. It is a lesson that, even with our cherished legal protections, terrible injustices are still possible. Yet the outcome has been favorable. These conforming, ambitious, and loyal Americans have overcome society's barriers and become successful by every standard. Their attitude to adversity has always been to try harder. Even the internment camp experience was used to good advantage. It was an opportunity to practice the roles needed to run a city and to care for themselves. Their soldiers became models of courage, sacrifice, and patriotism. The "unassimilable" have become examples for other minorities to follow.

CHAPTER 20
ITALIANS IN CALIFORNIA'S DEVELOPMENT
Domenico Ghiradelli, FatherJoseph M. Neri,
Andrea Sbarboro, Mark J. Fontana,
Antonio Cerruti, Joseph DiGiorgio, A. P. Giannini

JOE DIMAGGIO AND JOE MONTANA—great California sport figures. With the singers they probably come to mind first when we think of Italians in California. Of course, they are but some of the latest Italian settlers or their descendents. Italians arrived late to the California scene but have had a powerful influence on the State's development.

The first Italians came during the Mexican era. In 1822 Juan B. Bonifacio arrived on the ship John Begg at Monterey, where he settled and raised a family. Battisto Leandri landed in southern California the following year and became a storekeeper and judge.

Earlier an Italian in the Spanish Navy, Captain Alejandro Malaspina, made a round the world exploratory voyage from 1789 to 1794. He sailed up the Pacific coast from Acapulco to Alaska, looking for the Strait of Anian. Malaspina spend 12 days at the mission in Monterey in 1791. Paolo E. Botta, a ship's doctor and naturalist, traveled the California coast from San Diego to Fort Ross in 1827.

Many Italians tried their luck as miners during the Gold Rush. Most soon drifted into more stable occupations, like storekeepers, restauranteers, hotel keepers, gardeners, fishermen, farmers, and wine makers.

Domenico Ghirardelli

Domenico Ghirardelli was an exception. Originally he worked as a salesman, selling candy to miners. In 1851 he established a factory in San Francisco to make chocolates and liquers. This became the Ghirardelli Chocolate Company near Fisherman's Wharf, ultimately converted to the tourist attraction today known as Ghirardelli Square.

Father Joseph M. Neri

Italian priests of the Jesuit order established Santa Clara College, later Santa Clara University, in 1851. Saint Ignatius College, later San Francisco University, began in 1855. One of its priests, Joseph M. Neri, was a remarkable pioneer in the field of electricity, years before Edison invented the incandescent light in 1879. In 1874 Neri invented an electric light system using carbon filaments. That same year he devised a searchlight that could be seen for 200 miles. In 1876 Father Neri lit up Market Street in San Francisco, using arc lights of his invention.

The first waves of immigrants to California were mainly northern Europeans. They were English, Irish, Scotch, Welsh, Germans, and Scandinavians. By 1880 large numbers of southern Europeans—Italians, French, Spanish, Yugoslavians, Greeks—began coming. In 1880 15,000 Italians a day arrived in New York. The fare for passage from Italy was only $15. In 1898 Italian immigration exceeded northern European immigration. Most were from southern Italy. 500,000 persons left Italy in 1901. In 1913 one person in 40 left the country. This migration continued unabated until severely restricted in 1921. 15% to 20% of these people came West.

The attraction of America for poor, mostly illiterate Italians is not hard to see. During the 19th century France and Austria had occupied Italy. Most of the land was owned by the aristocracy. Farmers were renters, trying to work small plots of eroded, arid soil. Many families lived in one room houses with dirt floors without plumbing. Cholera and other infectious diseases ravaged the population. Famines were common, taxes high, the land overpopulated. Cheap or free land in the United States was a fantasy come true. The bonanza was sweetened by dreams of living in the West with cowboys and Indians—and release from the constrictions of ancient Italy.

Most Italians immigrants never got to California. They stayed in East Coast ghettos, suffering prejudice, limited opportunity, and tenement housing. Those that did come West found a more hospitable place with less prejudice and greater opportunity.

They usually followed their old skills in their new home, with its Mediterranean climate. Fishermen from southern Italy and Sicily thought they had found a new Adriatic or Mediterranean Sea. Their felucca boats with lateen sails crowded the North Beach wharf in San Francisco. In 1910 there were 700 boats manned by 2500 Italian fishermen.

Andrea Sbarboro,
founder of the Italian-Swiss
Agricultural Colony
in Sonoma County in 1881.

In the late 1800's northern Italians from Genoa, Turin, and Lombardia came in greater numbers. Wine making was their skill. The California climate and soil reminded them of home.

Andrea Sbarboro

In 1881 Andrea Sbarboro, formerly a Genoese banker and immigrant to California in 1852, established the Italian-Swiss Agricultural Colony in Sonoma County. The settlement was named Asti after a winemaking center in northern Italy. Sbarboro was an intellectual who had earlier started an Italian-American night school and written his own textbooks. He had studied utopian worker's colonies like those proposed by the social reformers John Ruskin and Robert Owen. Sbarboro bought 1500 acres near Cloverdale, hoping to settle 1000 immigrants there who would buy into the colony and make fine wine.

In many ways the dream came true. Sbarboro did establish the colony with poor Italian winemakers, and, as a business, it still exists. Stock was offered to the workers for their labor, but they didn't buy a share, preferring to be paid in cash.

The wine they made was excellent and sold well. Pietro Rossi was the winemaker. In 1897 the vintage was so large there were not enough barrels in California to hold it. Sbarboro ordered that a huge reservoir be dug in rock, the largest wine tank in the world, large enough to hold

500,000 gallons. Their wine was shipped to the East Coast in railroad tank cars and dominated the American wine market. Colony ceased to exist as a winery in 1988 after 101 years. It was absorbed into a larger firm.

Italians were also important vintners in southern and central California. In the 1880's Secundo Guasti established the "world's largest vineyard" in the Los Angeles area near Cucamonga. His Italian Vineyard Company specialized in making dessert wines.

The present giants in wine production are Ernest and Julio Gallo, centered in Modesto. Since World War II they have become the largest wine company in the United States, producing about 25% of the nation's wine.

Another giant is the Petri family. Fine winemakers in the Napa-Sonoma area include family wineries run by the Sebastiani's, Mondavi's, Martini's and many others.

Viticulture, of course, suffered a great blow during the years of Prohibition from 1919 to 1933, but many wineries survived by producing wine for church purposes, growing table grapes, or making substitute grape foods.

Mark J. Fontana, Antonio Cerruti, Joseph DeGiorgio

Italians were pioneers in the food processing plants of the State. Mark J. Fontana founded the California Fruit Packing Corporation (Calpac) in 1889. With another Italian, Antonio Cerruti, he began a line of canned goods now named Del Monte. Joseph DiGiorgio started farm work at age 14 for $8.00 a month. With his brother he eventually owned a huge acreage of food producing land scattered over several counties. They produced food for market from field to can under the S&W label. Northern Italians have dominated the state dairy farming industry with extensive ranching in the coastal areas.

A. P. Giannini

A. P. Giannini founded one of the country's largest banks. Born of a farm family in San Jose in 1870, he helped his stepfather merchandise farm produce. Eventually he established the bank that became the Bank of America. Loans to small farmers became his specialty. After the 1906 earthquake and fire Giannini rescued the two year old Bank of Italy's

Courtesy Wine Institute, San Francisco.

Cultivating a vineyard in the spring when this was still done with a horse and plow.

Picking the grapes at a Napa Valley vineyard in the late 1880s.

Courtesy Wine Institute, San Francisco.

Courtesy Wine Institute, San Francisco.

Pressing the grapes in a 1911 photograph.

Barrels of wine leave for storage in 1905.

Courtesy Wine Institute, San Francisco.

$300,000 capital by hiding it in two produce wagons and taking the money to his home in San Mateo. He was soon lending money to help rebuild San Francisco. His judgment and willingness to help small businesses created not only a great success for him but a new type of bank.

Many Italians have held public office. Angelo Rossi and Joseph Alioto have been mayors of San Francisco.

Italians have always had a strong artistic love. Soon after the Gold Rush began, many singers and traveling opera companies played to enthusiastic audiences in San Francisco and the new towns. The miners were appreciative if not always respectful. On Christmas Eve in 1909 Luisa Tetrazzini sang to an audience of 250,000, gathered in the streets of San Francisco near Lotta's Fountain (Chicken Tetrazzini was named for her). In 1919 the conductor of the visiting Naples San Carlo Opera Company, Gaetano Merola, organized the San Francisco Opera Association. Italian singers, popular and operatic, continue to please us all.

Italians have added a unique sparkle to California life. They have given much to the prosperity and happiness of all Californians, and life here has fulfilled many of their dreams.

A. P. Giannini, founder of the Bank of America.

Luisa Tetrazzini, opera diva, in a 1912 photograph.

177

CHAPTER 21
GERMANS MOLD DEVELOPING CALIFORNIA
Father E. F. Kino, John Augustus Sutter, Claus Spreckels

THE GERMAN ATTITUDE toward a developing America and California was somewhat different than other Europeans. More than most, they held on to their German roots, hoping to keep a separate existence. As a national group they were outnumbered only by the English and Irish as early American settlers.

The Germans came because of hard times at home, oppressive government, and the lure of free or cheap land in America. Although difficult to calculate, it has been estimated that Americans of German origin made up about 25% of the U.S. population in 1900. A 1979 study by the Bureau of Census reported 28.8% of Americans considered themselves at least partly of German ancestry, the largest national group. In 1900 Germans were the largest foreign born group in 27 states, including California.

Most immigrants wanted to lose their old ways and European culture as quickly as possible. America was the "melting pot". Many Germans felt differently. They were not frontiersmen and usually settled where there were others of their kind in an already populated area. In 1879 a German writer commented, "Germans can remain German in America: they will mingle and intermarry with non-Germans and adopt their ways, but they remain essentially German. They can plant the vines on hills and drink its wine with happy song and dance, they can have German schools and Universities, German art and literature, German science and philosophy..."

Large German colonies were established in Wisconsin, Missouri, and Texas. German continued to be spoken commonly and a German culture cultivated. As the country became more densely settled this separateness eroded. Unlike Mormons, Germans did not seek out unpopulated areas for themselves, and they were ultimately integrated into the culture of America. World War I, which pitted the U.S. against European Germans, was the end of the tendency to separateness. It then became apparent that German Americans had no real loyalty to the old country.

California, settled later than the American East and Midwest, experienced a milder form of this inclination. However, John Sutter dreamed of establishing a New Helvetia or German-Swiss colony, and there were other pockets of Teutonic settlers. What would have happened if Prussia had accepted Mexico's offer to sell Alta California for $6,000,000 in 1843? Because of their love of learning and culture, as well as their great energy, Germans have made great contributions to California.

Father E. F. Kino

Two Germans who never set foot in California were important in its development. Father Eusebius Francisco Kino was of great significance to early California exploration. He was born in Hala in the Tyrol of Germany. After studying at the Universities of Ingolstadt and Freiberg in Germany, he gained stature as a mathematician and was offered the position of mathematics professor at Ingolstadt. Instead, he become a Jesuit priest and missionary in Mexico.

Father Kino established the first mission in Baja California in 1683. He gained a reputation as a dynamic personage, missionary, educator, rancher, scientist, and explorer. Gentle and kindly as well as charismatic, he was the spiritual predecessor of the founder of the missions, Father Junipera Serra.

As an explorer, he investigated the land between Mexico and Arizona on both sides of the present border. His exploration of Lower California resulted in a convincing map in 1702 that put to rest the idea prevalent in the 17th Century that California was an island. Father Kino urged that others continue to explore the northern lands. After his time, the Spanish monarchy became fearful of the Jesuits' power and expelled them from Baja California in 1767. They were replaced by Franciscans, the order of Father Serra. Father Kino is remembered as a powerful motivator to others in the continued exploration of California.

The world-famous German explorer, Alexander von Humboldt, helped create an interest in California through his writings, though he never came closer than the archives library in Mexico City, which he

*John Sutter
advertised for immigrants
to come to his California empire.*

visited in 1804. Many places in California, including Humboldt Bay, are named in his honor.

Some of the first non-Spanish descriptions of the region were made by German scientists who came to California on Russian ships. In 1806 G.H. von Langsdorff wrote lengthy descriptions of Alta California in English and German after a visit of several months. Otto von Katzebue, a scientist, made visits to California on the Russian ship, Rurik. Another German member of the expedition, Adelbert von Chamisso, first described the California poppy.

John Augustus Sutter

It is hard to think of one individual who had a greater role in early California history than John Sutter. He was born in Germany and spent part of his childhood in Switzerland. He claimed to have been an officer in the Swiss Army. After being an unsuccessful merchant, he immigrated to the United States in 1834. Sutter soon decided to go West. He reached the West Coast by way of the Santa Fe Trail. After visiting Oregon and Hawaii, he came to California in 1839.

A kindly, friendly man, Sutter soon ingratiated himself with the Mexican authorities, who gave him a land grant of 50,000 acres on the

American River near present day Sacramento. Sutter dreamed of creating a New Helvetia (Switzerland). He built a fort and began an ambitious farming and trading community, using hundreds of Indians as serfs. For a time Sutter's plan seemed to have great promise. He bought Fort Ross from the Russians when they decided to leave California.

Many American craftsmen were attracted to the community. Sutter's Fort became the place for American immigrants, explorers, and ultimately soldiers and gold miners to restore and replenish themselves. When the American Bear Flaggers overthrew the Mexicans, Sutter sided with the Americans.

His operation, even before the Gold Rush, was overextended. He was land poor and had chronic difficulty in paying his bills. The Gold Rush began with the discovery of gold on his property. An employee, James Marshall, who was building a sawmill on the American River, discovered gold in January 1848. Soon Sutter's vast land holdings were overrun by gold seekers who squatted on his land. Sutter was bankrupt in 1852. He tried to reclaim his properties but was unable to finance the legal battles. For several years the California Legislature gave him a pension of $250 a month.

Sutter moved to a German colony in Pennsylvania to be close to Washington D.C., so he could lobby Congress in his various personal causes. Unsuccessful, he died penniless in 1880.

Sutter's name is given to a California county, the location of his Hock farm. His restored fort is now a museum in Sacramento.

Charles M. Weber

Charles Weber arrived in California in 1841 with the Bartleson-Bidwell party. He settled near San Jose, operated a successful store, and later manufactured shoes. He obtained a 50,000 acre land grant from the Mexican government in 1844, the site of a town called Tuleberg. During the Gold Rush it became an important regional business center and was renamed Stockton in 1848 in honor of Commodore Robert F. Stockton. Weber played an important role in the Mexican War as a cavalry officer.

A 1846 drawing of Sutter's Fort by Lt. J. W. Revere, U. S. Navy.

Claus Spreckels

The Spreckels family made news in California for many decades after Claus arrived in San Francisco from Germany in 1856. Before his rise in the business world he first worked as a grocery store helper. Sugar refining became his major interest. This led to raising sugar beets in California and sugar cane in Hawaii. Ship ownership was developed to get the sugar to California. Three of his four sons became newsmakers. John founded the Oceanic Steamship Company in 1881 carrying passengers and mail to Hawaii and New Zealand. He later published the *San Diego Union* and owned the city railroad in San Diego. He also owned the *San Francisco Call*. Rudolph became a prominent businessman and San Francisco political reformer. Adolph, enraged at charges made in the *San Francisco Chronicle* that his business practices were dishonest, shot the editor, M.H. de Young, in 1884. With his wife, he donated to San Francisco the magnificent art gallery, the California Palace of the Legion of Honor in 1924.

Germans as well as Italians played an influential role in developing the state's wine industry. The Wente family's winery was begun by father Carl and expanded by sons, Ernest and Herman. Charles Krug established an important winery in the Napa Valley. In southern California there was a cooperative winery in the German colony at Anaheim.

Many Germans became prominent in the motion picture industry in Hollywood. Refugees from Naziism who settled in the Los Angeles area included conductor Bruno Walter and novelist Thomas Mann.

Albert Bierstadt became the most famous illustrator of the western scene in the 19th Century. His massive pictures lend their commanding presence to major California museums. Other great German painters in California were Toby Rosenthal, C.C. Nahl, and H.W.A. Nahl.

CHAPTER 22
JEWS FIND FAVOR IN THE GOLDEN STATE
Levi Strauss, Samuel Goldwyn

THE VERY DAY COLUMBUS SET SAIL for the New World, Spain was expelling the Jews. By nightfall that day all Jews were ordered to be out of the country or be converted to Roman Catholicism. Who would have believed that 500 years later 40% of the world's Jews would live in the United States, or that a high proportion would be in California?

In colonial America many Jews were peddlers or small merchants selling cheap, useful articles. In the cities they sold notions (small items one might use in the home), or cigars, stationery, and jewelry. In the country the peddler struggled along from farm to farm, trying to sell clothing or dry goods from his backpack or cart. If business was good, he would rent a room at night. Otherwise, he slept on the ground. Life was hard and lonely. One salesman complained that for every customer there were 77 peddlers.

Jews migrated to California with other Americans in the 1840's and 1850's. Peddling was a temporary occupation that led to traditional merchandising from a store. Jews of the Gold Rush were merchants, not miners. Their specialties were clothing, dry goods, tobacco and jewelry. The clothing trade in California was almost entirely through Jewish stores or peddlers. Most of these merchants had come to California to escape oppression in Germany.

A network of stores was quickly established in the Gold Rush country. The Jewish immigrants came with their families, including relatives. A relative might start a new store with stock lent to him. Both local and Eastern bankers held an ingrained prejudice against extending credit to Jews. They overcame this difficulty by lending each other money and developing their own sources of credit. As honest merchants willing to accept a reasonable profit, the German-Jewish merchants prospered. Many became rich. By hard work and thrift they became respected members of the community.

Conditions in Germany improved by 1880, and the immigration of German Jews into the United States and to California declined to a trickle. But in 1881, Czar Alexander II of Russia was assassinated and the Jews were blamed for the murder. In revenge, harsh anti-Jewish pogroms (organized terror) began in Russia and its Polish province. In addition to physical violence, Jews were forbidden to live in major Russian cities and towns. School attendance was limited. They could not participate in the governement nor become lawyers. The situation became so terrible that more than a third of the Jews left Russia and Poland. During the next 50 years, two and a half million Russian and Polish Jews immigrated to the United States.

They were not accepted without question. The Eastern European Jews were culturally different from German Jews. They were peasants: coarse, uneducated and conspicous. Few had immediately saleable skills, except tailoring. The established German Jews feared the new arrivals would upset the hardearned approval they had enjoyed. Even so, B'nai B'rith, the Jewish fraternal organization, and a specially created agency, the Industrial Removal Office, helped the new immigrants find their way from the eastern seaboard cities to the population centers of the West.

Most Jews did well in California. Many had spectacular successes in business and politics and have been generous with their wealth. Merchants William Steinhart and Mortimer Fleishhacker helped found those San Francisco favorites, the Aquarium and Zoo. Mrs. Sigmund Stern donated the grove and outdoor auditorium named for her husband. The Haas family own the Oakland A's baseball team, recently the World's Champions but some years quite a public charity. Southern California Jews have been equally generous in funding cultural institutions of all kinds there. Norton Simon and Fred and Marcia Weisman have been major benefactors of art museums there.

Levi Strauss

Levi Strauss became the premier pants maker of the California goldminers. Born in Buttenheim, Germany in 1829, he immigrated to New York in 1847. His brother-in-law, David Stern, had established a dry

*Levi Strauss,
originator of a new kind
of work pants.*

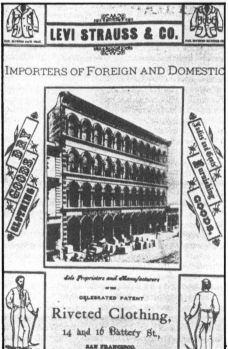

*An 1880 advertisement
for Levi Strauss
work clothes.*

goods business in San Francisco. In 1853, Strauss joined that firm, making the voyage around Cape Horn, and taking with him bolts of cloth. Most of his supplies were sold to passengers on the ship. When he arrived in San Francisco only some canvas was left, which was originally planned for tents and wagon covers.

Miners were complaining that their pants wore out too quickly from the rough work. Strauss had a tailor make the canvas into pants, which were soon accepted as extremely durable and called 'Levi's.' To produce a uniform color, he dyed the cloth indigo blue. A tailor in Carson City, Nevada, Jacob W. Davis, suggested that rivets on the corners of the pockets would add strength. He patented the idea with Strauss in 1873. The distinctive stitching on the pockets was added later.

Levi Strauss's little ideas, growing out of the desire to produce the best product possible, caused a major change in the clothing habits of the world. The 'waist overall' of the miners became the standard American work trouser; then wearing denims became a worldwide phenomenon. In time it came into common use by women and a popular garb for casual wear by both sexes.

Levi Strauss never married. Upon his death, management of Levi Strauss & Company passed to his four nephews. It remains in family ownership, managed by the Walter Haas family. The company continues to be based in San Francisco and manufactures a large line of work and leisure clothing for men and women, sold throughout the world. Annual sales are about 2.5 billion dollars. Recently the company moved into its new San Francisco quarters, Levi's Plaza.

Samuel Goldwyn

Motion pictures were invented in the 1880's. By the early 1900's a new industry had been created. The new form of entertainment moved from New York to southern California, and finally settled in Hollywood. From the beginning, making motion pictures was dominated by Jews. Jewish immigrants founded companies that for decades controlled 75% of the world's movie industry. Adolph Zukor, an Hungarian furrier, and Jessy Lasky, a glovemaker from Poland, began Paramount Pictures. Carl Laemmle, a bookkeeper, built Universal Pictures. William Fox, a garment maker, started 20th Century Fox. The Canadian brothers, Harry, Jack, Albert, and Sam Warner, created Warner Brothers. Russianborn Louis B. Mayer, with Sam Goldwyn, put together Metro-Goldwyn-Mayer.

Movie star Ronald Colman signs a 1926 movie contract as Sam Goldwyn stands by.

From the beginning of the industry, Samuel Goldwyn was a major figure in producing motion pictures. Born into a poor Jewish family in Warsaw, Poland, he was orphaned in early childhood. When eleven years old, he ran away to London. From there he went to Canada and entered the United States when he was thirteen. A Jewish family in the glove business in Gloversville, New York, put up his immigration fee and made him an apprentice in their factory.

Goldwyn couldn't get the knack of making gloves, but he convinced his benefactor to make him a salesman. Although only sixteen, he became a great success.

A biographer said that Goldwyn's lifelong traits were his refusal to acknowledge or accept rejection and his having an answer for every rejection.

Goldwyn was fascinated with the theater and decided to put his money into the new motion picture business. With his brother-in-law, New York vaudeville producer Jessy L. Lasky, and fledgling director Cecil B. DeMille, they made the first American full-length film, in 1913. It was made in eleven days at a cost of $30,000.

He made dozens of films before his death in 1974. Many early silent films were little more than brief recordings of hilarious or catastrophic situations. Goldwyn quickly realized that successful movies needed to

1938 movie poster of Sam Goldwyn's The Cowboy and the Lady. Not all his films were classics.

have good stories with sustaining interest. He also believed in quality and used first rate actors and writers. His film, "The Best Years Of Our Lives," won an Academy Award and became a film classic.

The great producer never stayed for long in any business situation with others. Seldom could he agree with partners. He soon left Metro-Goldwyn-Mayer, although his name remained on the corporate logo. To the end he remained an independent, finding his own financial sources.

Aside from his talents as a movie producer, he left the language enriched with many clever witticisms. "I'll give you a definite maybe," "Include me out," and "A verbal agreement isn't worth the paper it's written on" combine a play on his early difficulties with English and his incisive intelligence.

In 1971, he was awarded the Presidential Medal of Freedom, America's highest civilian honor.

The fate of Jewishness is unclear. In 1980 there were almost 6 million Jews in the United States. In 1988 there were an estimated 800,000 Jews in California Major concentrations are approximately 522,000 in Los Angeles, 140,000 in San Francisco-Oakland, and 25,000 in San Jose. Will devotion to Judiasm persist as a way of life, or will Jews, like other distinct groups, become assimilated into the American scene?

CHAPTER 23
THE SCANDINAVIAN MIGRATION
William Matson, John G. North,
Snowshow (John A.) Thompson

THE MAIN SURGE OF IMMIGRATION from the Scandinavian countries was from 1860 to 1930. Between 1893 and 1920, 1,250,000 Swedes, 850,000 Norwegians, 370,000 Danes, and 230,000 Finns came to the United States. After 1920 new immigration quota restrictions almost stopped the inflow of Scandinavians.

The winds of immigration are said to have 'push' and 'pull' forces. Strong economic forces in Scandinavia pushed young people away from their homes. The ancient custom of primogeniture dictated that the oldest son inherit his father's property. The younger sons of farmers might have stayed in a cottage on the family farm, rented land from another landowner, or rented forest land and created a small farm. But as the population grew, there were not enough farms in that agricultural society to go around. Then severe droughts and crop failures in Norway and Sweden during the 1860's brought people to near starvation. They mixed bark with flour for bread and ate lichens, moss, and roots.

In Denmark and Finland the political climate was oppressive. In 1864 Prussia (Germany) defeated Denmark in war. Over 150,000 Danes went under German rule, and young men were subject to conscription. In Finland, a province of Russia, conditions became very bad after Czar Alexander II was assassinated in 1881. Finns were forced into the Russian army. There was no free speech or assembly, and the police and politicians were Russian. Finland did not become an independent country until World War I.

The 'pull' factors working for immigration were also powerful. Land was cheap in the United States. A 160 acre farm could be purchased for $240 in the 1850's and 1860's. The forests and climate of the northern

191

tier of states was similar to the Scandanavian homeland. Immigrants who found land they liked wrote enthusiastic letters back home. These were handed about and printed in newspapers. The disappointed tended to be silent to hide their lack of success. Shipping companies had hundreds of agents in Europe who drummed up business for fares to the New World. The temperature of 'American fever' ran high.

In the 1870's wages were higher in America and living costs lower than in Scandanavia. Bricklayers earned $3.69 per day in Chicago versus $0.80 per day in Copenhagen; plasterers $3.30 per day versus $0.80; farm laborers $1.06 versus $0.36. Food was cheaper. There was a special demand for single housemaids and cooks. In Illinois they made $10.18 per month with a private room, board, and regular hours versus $2.50 per month in Denmark. California was very short of women. Those who went there quickly found husbands.

Most of the Scandanavian immigrants landed on the East Coast and worked their way west. Minnesota and Illinois were favorite states. In 1880 about 20% of the population of those states was Swedish; in California only 2% was Swedish.

The Scandinavian governments tended to favor emigration, to rid their countries of the poor and those without property. But there were also alarms that too many would emigrate, and not enough people would be left to do the work. Those that did leave were often criticized as lacking the character to face their problems. Some were considered traitors to their homeland, and many left home with bitterness.

Most of those who came to California were young, single men. After trying to make their fortune in mining, they settled into the trades they had known in Europe.

Sailing had long been an escape from the monotony and poverty at home. Scandinavians soon dominated coastwise and inland shipping on San Francisco Bay and its ports. The 'Scandinavian Navy' controlled the ships from captain to deckhand. A list of captains of the wooden and steel steamers of the California coast is full of Viking names—Ahlstrom, Arnesen, Bellesen, Benedikten, Bergersen, Bergmark, etc.

It took a master seaman to survive the storms and treacherous rocky northern California coast. There were few real harbors or docks and roads were scarce. The little ships could anchor close to the redwood lumber mills in the tiny 'dog hole' moorings. People, and everything they needed, went on the ships that brought lumber out to build California's cities.

In the forests of California those experienced as loggers found a situation to their liking. An advertisement in the *San Francisco Chronicle* of January 22, 1907, read:

TO THE SAWMILLS AND WOODS
WORK YEAR ROUND
BEAUTIFUL MENDOCINO
FREE FARE

The lumber towns had Scandinavian hotels for the newcomer's comfort. Finns especially liked this and in one area, Mendocino County, they were the largest foreign-born group in 1900. The men could work in the woods or the sawmills and save enough to realize their dream of buying cheap land for a farm in the nearby cut-over forest lands. A little farming on the cleared land became a second job. Making the huge stumps into railroad ties was another source of income. Few of these farms became self-supporting, but it was a better version of life than in the home country.

They tried new occupations, too. A Swedish colony south of Fresno at Kingsburg raised grapes to make raisins. This became the SunKist Raisin Growers. Another colony at Turlock, east of San Francisco, became famous for raising melons. Near Los Angeles, Solvang became a

A lumber steamer loads at Elk, Mendocino County, at the turn of the century.

Courtesy Flora Buchanan Collection, Kelley House Museum, Mendocino.

Captain William Matson, founder of the Matson Lines.

Courtesy of the Matson Lines, San Francisco.

Danish showplace. Founded in 1911 as a ranching, agricultural, and dairying community, the Danish architecture, folk school, and annual festival have made it a favorite tourist haunt.

Diverse California provided this group with new ways of life which were embraced with enthusiasm. Although their descendents have mostly left the pursuits of the original settlers, Scandinavians remain prominent in all aspects of California life.

William Matson

William Matson was born in Lysekil, a fishing town in Sweden. His parents were killed in an accident when he was very young, and at age 10 he went to sea as a handy boy. He arrived in California when he was 18 and decided to stay.

A person of legendary determination, in a few years Matson was a master mariner, then part owner of a small ship trading between California and the island of Hawaii. Manufactured goods were shipped to the Hawaiian Islands; sugar, pineapples, coffee, and hides were brought back. By 1901 he owned 7 ships. His sailing ships were replaced by oil burning steam ships.

The third Lurline goes under the Golden Gate Bridge.

Courtesy of the Matson Lines, San Francisco.

In 1902 Matson was the first shipping company to use wireless telegraphy in the Pacific. He also pioneered the use of gyro compasses and gyro pilots on his company's ships. To supply his ships with oil, he developed an oil field in California at Santa Maria with a pipeline to the coast.

The Matson Navigation Company was a major developer of the Hawaiian Islands. Matson realized the potential for tourism and built The Royal Hawaiian, SurfRider, Moana, and Princess Kaiulani hotels in the islands. A succession of five ships named *Lurline* (for Matson's daughter) carried tourists to Hawaii, Australia, New Zealand and the South Seas. Matson ships also carried troops and cargo in both World Wars.

William Matson died in 1917. The company was sold by the family in the 1960's. Passenger service ended in 1970. The Hawiian hotels were sold. In 1975 the opulent mansion and 600 acre estate, 'Filoli,' in Woodside (occupied by daughter Lurline and her husband, William P. Roth), was deeded to the National Trust for Historic Preservation. Grandson William Matson Roth bought and developed Ghirardelli Square in San Francisco in the mid-1960's.

John G. North

The Scandinavians also knew how to build ships, and the greatest shipbuilder in early Californai was John North. Trained as a shipwright and naval architect in Norway, North arrived in California in 1848. After a few years in the gold fields, he started his own shipyard in San Francisco in 1852. He built the first three-masted schooner on the Pacific Coast, and soon had a reputation as a builder of quality ships. By 1858 he had produced 120 hulls. During his career in California he built 53 bay steamers and 273 hulls.

His masterpiece was the *Chrysopolis*, built in 1860, to that date the largest ship built in California. It was 245 feet long, had a 40 foot beam and drew 10 feet of water. The ship's paddle wheels were 36 feet in diameter, powered by a one-cylinder 1357 horsepower engine. It carried 1000 passengers in splendor from San Francisco to Sacramento. The cabins had plate glass mirrors, marbletop tables, furniture upholstered in red plush, and were lit with brass lamps. On December 31, 1861, it set a speed record of 5 hours, 19 minutes, for the passage downriver from Sacramento to San Francisco. In 1875 the ship was rebuilt as a ferry for the San Francisco-Oakland run, and renamed the *Oakland*. It lasted 80 years until 1940, when it was destroyed by fire.

Sidewheeler, Chrysopolis, (Golden Gate) steams down the Sacramento River.

Courtesy Bancroft Library, University of California, Berkeley.

John North was a restless man. At the height of success he tired of his business and in 1865 returned to Norway, then toured the world. He returned to California, where he died in 1872 of a fever contracted in Honduras. He was 46.

Courtesy Bancroft Library, University of California, Berkeley.

Snowshoe (John A.) Thompson skis down the Sierras using a balance pole in 1856.

Snowshoe (John A.) Thompson

Another Norwegian, John Thompson, introduced skiing to the California Sierras. Born Jon Thoreson Rue in 1827 near Telemark, Norway, his father died soon after he was born. His mother married Thom Thomson and his family migrated to the American Midwest when he was ten. Thompson came to California from Wisconsin in 1851. For a while he tried gold mining, then in 1853 began what made him famous. For 20 years he ran a private mail delivery service during the winters from Placerville to Carson Valley, on the eastern slope of the Sierras in Nevada.

197

He carried a pack weighing 60 to 80 pounds over a 90 mile route. The charge was $2.00 a letter. At times other freight was put on the pack.

The idea for using skis, which Thompson called snowshoes, came from his childhood memories of their use in Norway. The skis were 7 1/2 feet long, 6 inches wide, fastened by a single strap. Thompson was about six feet tall and weighed about 180 pounds. He usually travelled at night to prevent warm snow from sticking to the undersurface of the skis. Although there were few roads, he could travel about 40 miles in a day. He wore a heavy wool jacket but never carried a blanket. Often he slept under trees or in caves. He was never frostbitten.

The Carson Appeal of May 15, 1876, described him as "Possessed of Herculean strength, with nerves of steel and an iron will, and a heart susceptible of the kindest feeling, he was at once the beau ideal of strong manhood." Using a single balance pole, he must have been a sight, gliding down the untracked mountain slopes.

Thompson gained little but publicity for his exploits. The major motivation for his mail carrying appeared to be the satisfaction he got from not only providing mail service, but carrying medicines and rescuing the stranded. Never given a U. S. Mail contract, he had to work as a laborer during the summers. He died at age 49, remembered as a unique and humanitarian athlete.

The Norwegian polar explorer, Roald Amundsen, finally found and sailed through the Northwest Passage in a voyage lasting from 1903-6. He sailed his 47 ton converted fishing sloop, *Gjoa*, through the northern Canadian islands at 71° North latitude, around the north coast of Alaska, and into the Pacific Ocean. The ship was then sailed down to San Francisco, where for decades it was on display in Golden Gate Park. Recently the *Gjoa* was returned to Oslo, Norway, where it is displayed as a national treasure. Amundsen was a true Voyager to California.

CHAPTER 24
SOME SMALLER GROUPS COME TO CALIFORNIA: VOYAGERS FROM FRANCE, PORTUGAL AND ARMENIA
Paul Masson, Manuel Silveira d'Andrate, Hagop Seropian

THE GOVERNMENT OF FRANCE was interested in Alta California and sent naval expeditions to study that distant land. Jean Francis De Galaup, Count of La Perouse, was the first northern European visitor to Alta California after Francis Drake. He commanded a French scientific mission that explored the Pacific coast from Alaska to Monterey in 1785. His two ships with their experts made note of the geography, geology, climate and botany of California during a ten day visit. Their findings were published in a book in 1787. La Perouse felt that the Spanish missionaries had good intentions but used harsh methods to control the Indians.

Other French scientific missions, in 1827-28 and 1837-38, were led by August B. Duhaut-Cilly and Cyrille P. T. Laplace. Eugene D. De Mofras visited California in 1841-42 as an attache to a Mexican government party of inspection. He concluded that the territory would probably be annexed by a major country in the near future.

The first Frenchman to settle in Alta California was Jean L. Vignes, who is thought to have come in 1831. He brought grape cuttings from his native Bordeaux and established a vineyard in what is now downtown Los Angeles. Vignes became a wealthy businessman and social leader. Two nephews, Jean Vignes and Pierre Sansevain, joined him in the business and also became important early California personages.

Jean J. Vioget was an early settler in Yerba Buena during the pre-American era. He came with his own ship in 1837. Trained as an artist and surveyor, he mapped Yerba Buena and John Sutter's inland empire.

A rush of French immigrants came because of the Gold Rush and a new revolution in France in 1848. France had tried another monarchy from 1830-48 in the person of King Louis Philippe. Bad economic conditions disillusioned the poor, and the government was brought down in a series of riots. Famines and epidemics of cholera added to the unrest. Battles with the police caused over 12,000 deaths and many more arrests. The new government, wanting to rid the country of troublemakers, urged emigration to California when news of the gold strike there was heard in France.

The French may have suffered from more incorrect information about the gold fields than most other Argonauts. Gold supposedly abounded in an area 800 miles long and 100 miles wide. It came in many forms-- as dust, nuggets and rocks. Enthusiasm was dampened some by dark rumors of greed turning ordinary folk into assassins. Still, it was said that enormous profits were easy to make. Promotors of the immigrant companies leaving for California advertised that shares could be bought with confidence by anyone.

Of course, the reality was different. The companies disbanded as soon as they arrived in California, when everyone rushed off to the gold fields forgetting past promises to work together. Most people had such poor luck in finding gold that by 1850 the French public had lost most of its interest in the Gold Rush.

About 10,000 men had come from France and perhaps 25,000 people of French origin were in California during the 1850's. Most of them settled into banking, merchandising, wine making and other steady pursuits.

Francois L. A. Pioche arrived in San Francisco in 1849. Soon he was a powerful businessman and built San Francisco's first block of business buildings. His wharves, Market Street railroad, and gas works were also the first of their kind. Other real estate promotions were the development of Hayes Valley, Visitation Valley and Mission Dolores Valley in San Francisco. Financial reverses apparently caused him to commit suicide in 1875.

Two French retailers started large department stores in San Francisco that lasted until the 1960's. Raphael Weill established The White House and Felix Verdier created The City of Paris, both large popular stores.

French Hospital survives in San Francisco from the early French colony's efforts to care for the health needs of all citizens.

*Paul Masson
strikes an
aristocratic pose.*

Courtesy Paul Masson Vineyards.

Paul Masson

The personification of French elan was Paul Masson, master of the Paul Masson Vineyards near Saratoga. Born into a family of wine makers in Burgundy, he was 19 when he came to California in 1878. The vineyards of countryman Charles Le Franc near San Jose reminded Paul of Burgundy and he began working there as a winemaker. Then he married the boss's daughter and established his own vineyards and winery, specializing in fine champagne as well as other wines.

Masson played the transplanted benign French aristocrat. In the La Cresta Vineyards he built a fabulous chalet as his home. The winery was embellished with a doorway from a 12th Century European church.

201

He played host to the famous. His wines and champagne won medals on a worldwide basis. A genial, imposing person, Masson became a spokesman for California wine that won respect everywhere. The legendary Frenchman in pince-nez and striped pants was dubbed the Duc de Cognac by his friends.

But Prohibition brought hard times and the establishment was sold in 1936. In 1940 Paul Masson's long, happy life ended, when he was over 80. Wines are still sold under the Paul Masson name and the La Cresta Vineyards and Winery are the site of the Paul Masson Summer Series of music concerts.

*

The earliest expeditions to Alta California were led by Portugese. Juan Rodriquez Cabrillo, his pilot Bartolome Ferrelo, and Sebastian R. Cermeno were all Portugese working for the Spanish crown.

Immigration of the Portugese to California was tied to the whaling industry, although they were famous as farmers and fishermen in their adopted home. Most of the early Portugese immigrants came from the Azores, nine Atlantic islands about 900 miles west of the mother country. These islands were settled during the great days of Portugese exploration during the 1400's.

Life was cruel on the little islands. Most of the land was owned by the aristocracy and farming brought meagre crops. Prospects for a young man were bleak. One of the few chances for a better life was to become a sailor and emigrate to America or Hawaii.

Whale hunting during the first half of the 19th Century was a big business. Oil derived from petroleum taken from the ground was only beginning to be developed. Whale blubber was an important source of oil. The fat was cooked in large kettles on the whaling ships, stored in barrels, and usually returned to the ship's home port in transport ships. The bones of the whales were also salvaged, for use as flexible reinforcing material in clothing.

New Bedford, Massachusetts was the capitol of the American whaling industry. In 1845, 685 whaling ships registered there as their home port. Voyages on these ships often lasted three or four years, with the hunts extending into the region of the Hawiian Islands and the north Pacific Ocean.

Manuel Silveira Andrade,
Portugese immigrant
to California in the 1860s.

Manuel Silveira d'Andrate

In 1859, at age 18, Manuel d'Andrade left his home on the Azorean island of Faial to work as a carpenter on the neighboring island of Flores. There he signed on as a sailor on the New Bedford ship, *Bark Pacific*, bound for the Pacific Ocean with Jacob A. Howland as Captain.

They unloaded 110 barrels of sperm oil in the Azores rendered from whales killed in the Atlantic Ocean on the voyage from New Bedford. A stop was made at Faial, but Manuel was refused permission to go ashore to say goodbye to his parents and friends. Seven months later they anchored in Maui, Hawii, after making the dangerous passage around Cape Horn. They had 1100 barrels of whale oil and 7500 pounds of whale bone. Irish and sweet potatoes were taken aboard. Then the ship headed for the north Pacific. When it returned to Honolulu the *Bark Pacific* had killed 52 whales, made 3700 barrels of oil, and salvaged 24,000 pounds of bones.

After two years and two months on the ship, Manuel decided that he had had enough of the sailor's life. He went to the American Consul in

203

Honolulu, paid for another sailor to take his place for the remainder of the voyage, and took passage to San Francisco, arriving there on December 4, 1861.

He resumed his work as a carpenter and became a leader in the Portugese community, which centered its activities in nearby San Leandro. Manuel married Rosario Geraldina Fagundes, who was born on his native island in the Azores. In 1874 he became an American citizen. His descendents continue to live in California, where he died in 1916.

Many Portugese sailors stayed in Hawaii and worked as laborers there. In 1884, only the Chinese were a larger foreign born group there. Many of them migrated to California in the next few decades and settled in the San Leandro area where they became reknowed as farmers and dairymen. J.B. Avila, another native of the Azores, introduced the sweet potato to California. Portugese sailors were influential in developing the tuna catching and canning industry in southern California.

*

Armenian emigration to the United States came as a direct result of persecution in their homeland. A distinct political entity for 3000 years, Armenia was absorbed into Turkey in 1375. Under the Ottoman Turks the Armenians were seen as a troublesome minority. The Turkish government conducted systematic massacres not only against Armenian men but also the women and children in their villages. The main cause of the conflict was religious. The Armenians were Christians and the Turks Moslem. It is also said that the Armenians were hated because of their progressive ways, shrewdness in business, and devotion to universal education. There were major massacres in 1894, 1895, 1896, 1908, and 1915.

Immigration to America was encouraged by the long association of Armenians with American Christian missionaries. The first immigrants in number came to the United States in the 1870's. In 1874 the first Armenian, Frank Normart, came to California. He was a farm machinery salesman who soon returned to the East coast.

Hagop Seropian

In 1879 the first of the five Seropian brothers, Hagop (or Jacob), came to the Fresno area. He was sickly and wanted to improve his health. Soon his four brothers joined him and found that the climate reminded them of Armenia. Letters home encouraged others to come. In 1883, 43 more Armenians arrived in the Fresno area.

Courtesy Armenian Film Foundation, Thousand Oaks, California.

A family picture of the Seropian family. Hagop (Jacob) Seropian is
second from the left. To his right is his father, to his left his two brothers.

The Seropian family started a fruit peddling business, selling their
wares from a wagon. Then they expanded their business and began to
ship dried figs to the Middle West. In 1894 they led a brief revolt
against high rail freight rates by hauling their figs from Fresno to San
Francisco in their own mule-drawn wagons.

Produce native to Armenia flourished in the Fresno area. The Smyrna
fig, Armenian cucumber, and Kassaba melon were introduced and became part of the American diet. The brothers branched out into fruit
growing. Watermelons became an Armenian specialty.

Fresno has become the center of Armenian settlement in California,
followed by Los Angeles. In 1918 there were over 18,000 such settlers
in the Fresno area.

Other important activities of this group are their domination of the
Oriental rug business in the state and their prominence in the arts. Haig
Patigian, born in Armenia, became a famous California sculptor. Rou-
ben Mamoulian found prominence as a movie director. Probably the
most famous Armenian in the arts is William Saroyan. The writer was a
second generation Armenian who suffered much deprivation as a child.

205

William Saroyan,
Armenian-American writer,
in the 1930s.

George Deukmejian,
Armenian-American,
Governor of California.

His father died and because of poverty his mother placed him in an orphanage for several years. He quit school when he was twelve and became a messenger boy. During the 1930's he became a writer and soon produced numerous nationally acclaimed plays, novels and short stories. Saroyan's most famous work, the play, "The Time of Your Life," (for which he received the Pulitzer Prize) was written in 1939. Many of his works had a flamboyant, adventurous, fun-loving quality which seemed to be missing in his personal life, which ended in 1981.

George D. Deukmejian has become the most important Armenian political figure. Elected Governor of California in 1982, he was re-elected for a second term.

CHAPTER 25
THE OKIES MAKE IT TO CALIFORNIA
Woody (Woodrow Wilson) Guthrie

ROUTE 66, NOW INTERSTATE 40, snakes its way to Los Angeles through Little Rock, Oklahoma City, Amarillo, Albuquerque, Flagstaff, Barstow and a lot of dusty towns in between. During the 1930's this was the route taken to their promised land to escape poverty by people collectively called "Okies".

Like most great social events, several forces converged to create their problem. One cause of this migration was drought and dust storms in the states of Kansas, Arkansas, Oklahoma, Missouri and Texas. That area became known as the Dust Bowl, because of the dramatic dust storms that passed over the parched land. The Okie migration to California had begun before the dust storms, in the 1920's. The Depression of the 1930's greatly increased farm poverty. Drought and dust made it worse. Generations of poor farming methods had exhausted the land. The federal government, in trying to help rural poverty and low crop prices, had encouraged crop acreage restrictions. Landlords realized that tractors and other farm machinery made their sharecropping tenants expendable and began to evict them.

The poorest members of that society decided to move West, to try their luck in California. They put their wives, children, and belongings into jalopies and drove west on Route 66. This group was different than earlier immigrants; it was a massive movement of white American citizens. Most of these families had been in the country for six or seven generations.

The Okies knew how to pick cotton and many stopped in Arizona, where they were welcomed. In the early 1930's they could also pick cotton in California. California farming was different than what they'd done before. In the great Central Valley farms were immense. An army

A family of Okies and their car near Wascò, California.

Courtesy Bancroft Library, University of California, Berkeley.

of workers was needed but only to thin and harvest crops. Mexican braceros and gangs of Filipinos worked in the fields during the 1920's. They had replaced the earlier Chinese, Japanese, Hindu, Portugese, and Italians. The Mexicans, however, caused a problem because they needed relief support during the off season. Employers encouraged them to return to Mexico for part of the year by paying their fare. The system had not been fine tuned. Some years a labor shortage developed when too many workers stayed in Mexico.

The land owners saw the Okies as a solution to their problem, an army of cheap migrant farm laborers, and encouraged them to move west.. Advertisements promised ample farm work in California. Critics said this deception was intended to drive down labor costs. The Okies, having nothing, were glad to work for 25¢ an hour. It was more than they had earned at home.

The trip across country had been hard but full of hope. A poem of the day says:

> "Don't let anyone fool you and lead you in to harm,
> For you sure can't make a living on a forty acre farm.
> So when I see Old Texas one thing I truly hope,
> It will be from California through a long range telescope."

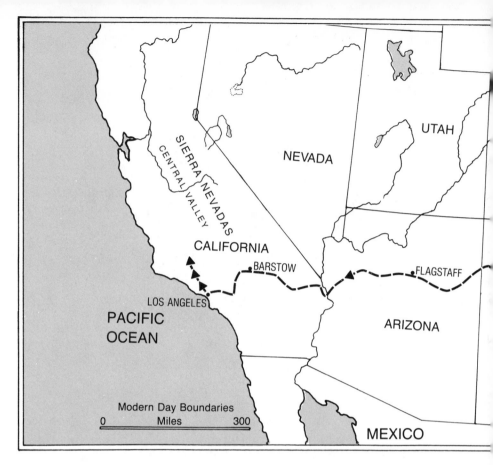

But unlike Mexicans, who didn't want to join settled American society and who disappeared when the harvest was over, Okies didn't see
themselves as migrants. They wanted to settle down, own land, and find
a place at the California table.

The new arrivals had no money, no regular jobs, and no place to stay.
They clustered with their friends along the irrigation ditches outside the
towns of the Central Valley. "Little Oklahomas" sprang up as shanty
towns. Winter rains made them all the more squalid.

The Depression wore on and the Okies were not longer seen as a solution to California's farm problem, but as a problem themselves. The
migration of 300,000 destitute white farmers from the south-central
United States caused shock and fear in their adopted home. Then the
government cut back farm production and paid growers not to use their
land. With several workers available for every farm job, the growers cut
wages in order to increase profits.

Starvation wages kept the worker's resentment boiling. Attempts to
unionize the workers brought strike breaking, and labor leaders were all

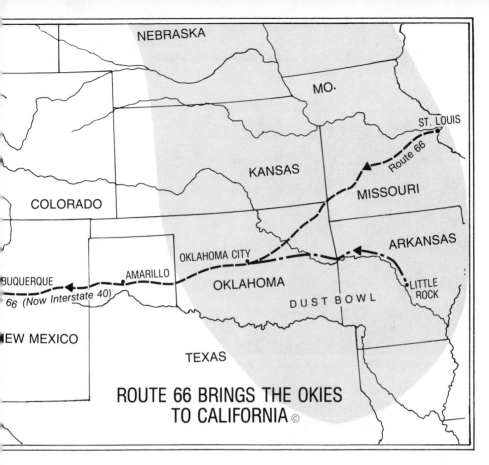

NEBRASKA

MO.

ST. LOUIS

Route 66

KANSAS

MISSOURI

COLORADO

ARKANSAS

OKLAHOMA CITY

AMARILLO

OKLAHOMA

LITTLE
ROCK

BUQUERQUE

66 (Now Interstate 40)

DUST BOWL

EW MEXICO

TEXAS

ROUTE 66 BRINGS THE OKIES
TO CALIFORNIA ©

accused of being communists. The Okies made heavy demands on local county governments for needed medical, educational, and welfare services. California law required a year's residence before anyone was eligibile for aid. The hope was that the migrants would leave the state.

Even the cities became economically strained by these problems. In 1936 Los Angeles decided to act. The Los Angeles Police Chief directed 150 officers to block the major points of entry into California used by migrants. These officers were stationed at places remote from Los Angeles, like Crescent City and Blythe. Using vagrancy laws, single, unemployed males were fingerprinted and arrested if they tried to enter the state. These procedures lasted for only a few weeks, as they were clearly unconstitutional. United States citizens could not be prevented from moving about in their own country. There was, however, some amusement concerning Chief Davis. Nevada erected a sign near Reno reading, "Stop! Los Angeles City Limits!" The Los Angeles Police Chief backed off, saying he was only trying to find criminals.

A farm in Oklahoma during the Dust Bowl days.

Desolate Main Street of Cadds, Oklahoma in 1938.

The state and federal governments entered into a battle over what to do about the Okies. The especially rainy winter of 1938 made the migrant's suffering even worse. Conservatives saw the Okies as "degenerate, degraded losers" and didn't want the federal government to make relief money or jobs available immediately to the migrants.

A liberal governor was elected in California in 1938, but his efforts to help the migrants were blocked by conservative elements in the State Legislature. In 1940 California relief laws were made even stricter by requiring three years residence before state aid could be received. If conditions were made bad enough, it was hoped the Okies would leave California.

In 1939 the Okies' plight was brought to the attention of the national public. John Steinbeck, a California novelist who used social issues in his books, wrote **The Grapes of Wrath**. The story describes a destitute Oklahoma family, the Joads, who decide to find a new farm in California. They pack their old car with their scant possessions and head west on Route 66. A succession of calamities, including the death of the grandparents, near starvation, dashed hopes for steady employment, and harrassment by local police, fail to shake the family's unity. The book ends with no prospect of a happy outcome.

The trials of this likeable, poor but honest family brought an outcry of sympathy across the nation. California, however, was not so accepting of the book. Steinbeck was accused of being a communist sympathizer and an inept writer. Valley counties were indignant because he failed to give any credit for their efforts to help the migrants. However, the author won the Pulitzer Prize for **The Grapes of Wrath** and wrote other great novels. He was awarded the Nobel Prize for literature in 1962.

World War II rather quickly solved the problem of the Okies. Jobs became plentiful. The Okies didn't want to be migrant farm workers and these jobs went back to the Mexicans. The Okies disappeared into the general population. Tom Joad left the pages of history and literature when he found a defense job in the city.

Woody (Woodrow Wilson) Guthrie

Woodrow Wilson Guthrie, born in 1912, was the balladeer of the Okies and the most important folk singer of his day. At age 15 he ran away from his home in Okemah, Oklahoma and became a hobo and migrant

*Woody Guthrie,
balladier of the Okies.*

Courtesy Woody Guthrie Publications, Inc.

worker. Riding freight trains west, Guthrie joined the Okie migration. His genius was in catching the spirit of Okie culture, to express it in his songs, which he played on the harmonica and guitar. He wrote over 1000 songs and helped create the Folk Music rage of the 50's and 60's. His was the voice of the dispossessed, and he became a folk hero for the Depression's migrant poor. Two of his classic songs are "So Long, It's Been Good To Know Ya," and "This Land Is Your Land," the latter the signature song of the 1960's civil rights movement.

Guthrie's end came tragically, from Huntington's Disease, a rare hereditary disease that causes mental deterioration in middle age, then finally death. He died in 1967. His widow, Marjorie, has promoted understanding of the disease, and has solicited funds for research into its cause. Their son, Arlo, is a well-known entertainer.

CHAPTER 26
THE OTHER ASIANS:
CALIFORNIA SETTLERS FROM ASIAN COUNTRIES
OTHER THAN JAPAN AND CHINA
Joyce Luther Kennard

AMERICA'S RISE AS A SUPERPOWER and its wars in the Orient during the last hundred yeas have encouraged migration from a number of countries across the Pacific Ocean. Many of these immigrants preferred to settle on the West Coast, especially in California. They have become the country's fastest growing legal minority. In the past 20 years over 40% of the immigrants to America have been Asian. Mainly they are new citizens from the Philippines, Korea, Vietnam, Kampuchea (Cambodia), and Laos.

Koreans first came in 1882 after a trade and friendship treaty was signed with their country. Laborers were needed in the sugar cane fields and pineapple plantations of Hawaii after Chinese immigration stopped because of the Chinese Exclusion Act of that year. A new immigration law in 1924 stopped Korean immigration. The Korean War of 1950-53 brought a new stream of Korean refugees and brides of American servicemen and their relatives to this country. In 1980 there were almost 160,000 Koreans in California.

The Spanish-American War of 1898 freed the Philippine Islands from Spanish rule and they were made a protectorate of the victorious United States. Filipinos gained American citizenship and were free to come to the United States without restriction. In 1934 the United States gave future independence to the Philippines but cut off immigration. Filipinos once again became aliens. The Philippines continued as a Navy and Army base of the United States, leading to many marriages with American servicemen. The islands were a major battleground of World War II. In 1946 the Philippine Republic came into being.

Many Filipinos first came as farm laborers in Hawaii before moving on to the mainland. In 1965 immigration quotas were expanded greatly, and the flow of immigrants resumed. More recent immigrants tend to be better educated and work in professional occupations. There are now some 490,000 Filipinos in California, more than any other Asian group, including Chinese and Japanese.

The bloody Vietnam War put American troops into South Vietnam to help their ally fight the invading North Vietnam army. American involvement in the war lasted from 1961 to 1975 and spread to some extent into neighboring Laos and Kampuchea. At one time 550,000 U. S. servicemen were there. Over 50,000 died.

700,000 people from the area have come to the United States as refugees or immigrants. Over 265,000 Vietnamese have settled in California. When the U.S. left Vietnam, we wished to protect our friends there and gave refugee status to many South Vietnamese, with permission to emigrate to the United States. Many servicemen had married during

Vietnamese refugee children in a Malaysian camp in 1979.

Courtesy United Nations.

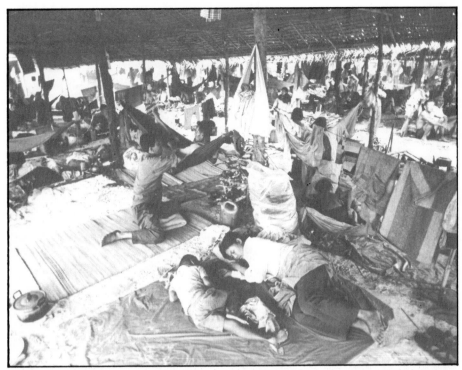

A Thailand refugee camp in 1979 for displaced Southeast Asians.

their stay in Vietnam. The first group to leave Vietnam after the fall of the government were American servicemen's wives and their relatives, government officials and other American collaborators, South Vietnam army officers and their families, and other friends of our government. It was feared that they would be killed by victorious North Vietnam. This group spoke English, was better educated, came from the professional and managerial class, and was accustomed to life in a more highly developed society. With furious energy they have become restaurant operators, retailers and businesspeople of all kinds.

Citizens of Kampuchea fled a conquering government that killed a third of its population. Laos was also scourged by fanatical communism. Streams of people became refugees looking for any place in the world that would take them. Many of these uneducated farmers and fishermen became the 'Boat People.' They took to sea in overcrowded boats, often without adequate provisions or seafaring experience, hop-

Refugees in Malaysia affirm their acceptance of immigration to the United States.

ing to find a friendly port or ship at sea. Many died from the perils of the ocean or were even killed by pirates. Others fled overland to Thailand. They were gathered into refugee camps in Asia, then redistributed throughout the world. California has taken more than any other state. Unprepared for their new life in a completely different culture, a high percentage continue to live on public welfare.

California will surely be changed by this new group of citizens. As fewer immigrants come from Europe, Asians and Hispanics take center stage. Almost half of the new population growth will come from Orientals. Since 1965, 20,000 new immigrants a year are allowed from each country. There is no limit for those who can be admitted as refugees. New citizens are able to bring their relatives into the United States by advancing them on the immigration quota list, making a 'family chain' migration process.

These newly arrived Asians have not met the intense rejection and discrimination experienced by the Chinese and Japanese a century ago, and most of them are doing well in their new home. The new immigrants try very hard to fit in. Some complaints are heard that they do not speak English but continue to speak their native language in their homes. In southern California they often cluster in ghettos of their own kind. There is a resistance to assimilation by many. Old time residents resent Oriental signs sprayed across the business districts of whole towns. Some of the refugee youth have become severe social and educational problems. Having lived for years in camps often without families or any feeling of allegiance to society because of their harsh past, hopelessly behind educationally, they have little interest in the ways of traditional society.

These new citizens hold their own in most ways. They are extremely industrious. Although as a group they earn lower wages then the average American and more live below the poverty line, family income is higher because more people in the family work. Their lower income reflects their newness to the country.

A high premium is placed on education and the development of professional skills. Compared to the rest of the population, they are better educated, and more of them find their way into the professions and managerial jobs. In time this can only lead to their assuming a leading role in society. Their children have become extremely successful students. In the 1990 Westinghouse science talents search for high school students, three out of four were Asian-Americans.

Joyce Luther Kennard

When Joyce L. Kennard was appointed to the California Supreme Court in 1989, a great story of personal achievement began another chapter. The 47 year old immigrant from Indonesia became the first Asian to sit as a justice in the State's highest court.

She was born in Indonesia during World War II with a Dutch father and an Indonesian mother. Her father died when she was an infant, and she and her mother were interned in West Java. After the war her mother worked as a typist and they lived in a segregated section of their town in New Guinea in a hut without indoor plumbing. She did not use a telephone nor see television until she was 14. They moved to the Netherlands, where she went to high school. A severe infection cost her one of her legs and she wears a prosthesis.

219

Joyce Luther Kennard,
California immigrant
from Indonesia
and 1989 appointee
to the California
Supreme Court.

When she was 20 she emigrated to Los Angeles where she worked as a secretary. Enrolling first in Pasadena City College with $ 5,000 inherited from her mother, Joyce Kennard later attended the University of Southern California on scholarships and attained degrees in public administration and law. After her graduation she worked as a Deputy Attorney General and as an attorney for the State Court of Appeals. In 1986 she was appointed a municipal judge in Los Angeles. There was a quick advancement to superior court judge and appellate court justice.

Called by some the 'Model Minority,' Asians are a long way from dominating California life either by numbers or position. In 1990 the combined population of Californians of Asian descent will be about 8.5% of the entire state population. Their character and prospects give them influence far beyond their numbers.

CONCLUSION
CALIFORNIA'S CONTINUING TRANSFORMATION
A FUTURE HARD TO FATHOM

In a world shrunk by instant communication and cheap transportation, everyone knows about bountiful California. The state has become a favored place in the whole world to move to, and Southern California is usually the first choice. Movies and television world-wide show Los Angeles as a balmy, palm tree forested paradise. Most new immigrants come from warm weather countries in Latin America or Southeast Asia, so Southern California's weather is an added bonus, reminding them of home. Los Angeles has become a city of minorities, as has San Francisco.

This babel of strange voices can be threatening. One elementary school in Los Angeles reports that 95% of entering students speak no English. Over 80 different languages are spoken in Los Angeles County. Operators on the emergency telephone number 911 frequently can't even guess the language spoken to them.

In the short 200 years since California was colonized by outsiders, the only sure feature has been change. The Spanish era is now only a romantic memory. Although New England-style Americanization seemed inevitable and permanent, that was diluted by other types of immigrants. Hispanic influences have surged back in recent years. A new wave of Orientals reinforces the marks those people introduced a hundred years ago.

The touch of each group is different. Each voyager has his private dream. Still, California does not splinter, and it stays on the leading edge of America's development. It continues to be attractive because of its climate, healthy economy, and tolerance for all peoples. Most important is the belief that the future, though uncertain, will probably be good.

Index

A

Acapulco, Mexico, port of Manila galleons, 57, 60
African Americans in California, 141-150
Alaska, Russian occupation, purchase from Russians, 79
Alder Creek, winter site for some of Donner Party, 117
Aleuts, sea otter hunters for Russians, 77, 78
Alioto, Joseph, Mayor of San Francisco, 176
Alta California, Upper and later American California, 36, 38, 39, 68
Alvarado, Juan Bautista, nephew of Gen. Mariano G. Vallejo, 123
American River, where gold was discovered at Sutter's Mill, 99, 154
Americans in early California, 19, 83-87, 99-119
Amundsen, Roald, Norwegian explorer, discovered Northwest Passage, 198
Angel Island in San Francisco Bay, immigration port of entry for Asians, 157
Anglos in California, 120
Anza, see de Anza, Juan Bautista
Argonauts, name for gold seekers, 11, 99
Arguello, Dona Conception, daughter of early Commandant of San Francisco, 77, 78
Armenians in California, 204-207
Asti, home of Italian-Swiss Agriculture Colony, 172, 173
A Thousand Mile Walk to the Gulf, book by John Muir, 131
Avila, J. B., Portugese immigrant who introduced sweet potatoes to California, 204
Azores Islands, home of many Portugese immigrants to California, 202, 203
Asians in California, 151-160, 161-169, 215-220
Aztec Indians in Conquest of Mexico, 33-35

B

Baja California, Lower or Mexican California, 35, 36
Bank of America, 173, 176, 177
Bank of Italy, later Bank of America, 173, 176
Baranoff, Alexander, Russian official in Alaska, 77
Battle of San Pascual of Mexican War, 82, 84
Bear Flag, flag of Republic of California, 83
Bear Flag Revolt, establishes Republic of California, 82, 83, 87, 123
Beckwourth, James P., early black explorer, 144
Benicia, city of, 87, 124
Benton, Jessie, wife of John Charles Frémont, 91
Benton, Thomas Hart, U.S. Senator, father of Jessie Benton, 91
Bent's Fort, Colorado, frontier fort, 97, 98
Bering, Vitus, Danish-Russian explorer, 77
Berry, James Richard, early Irish settler, 135
Bidwell, John, led first wagon train into California, 113-116, 120
Bierstadt, Albert, German-American painter of early California, 183
Blacks in California, 141-150
B'nai B'rith, Jewish fraternal organization, 185
"Boat People", 157, 217, 218

C

D

E

F

Fort Ross, headquarters of Russians in California, 77-79
Fort Snelling, U.S. fort in Minnesota Indian Territory, 111
Fort Vancouver, Oregon, English fort on Columbia River, 92, 95, 110
Fox, William, Jewish movie maker, 187
Frémont, John Charles,
     American explorer, military commander, politician, 82-85, 90-98
French in California, 199-200
Fresno, city of, 204, 205

G

galleons, Spanish transport ships, 49-50, 55-61
Gallo, Ernest, vintner, 173
Gallo, Julio, vintner, 173
Galvez Expedition, establishes California missions, 68-76
General Grant National Park, 132
"Gentlemens' Agreement of 1908," bars Japanese immigration to U.S., 164
Germans in California, 178-183
Ghirardelli, Domenic, Italian-American businessman, 170
Giannini, A. P., Italian-American banker, 173, 176, 177
Gila Trail, 98
Gilroy, John, early Scotch settler, 126
Golden State, name for California, 151
"Golden Mountains," early Chinese term for Gold Rush California, 151, 160
Gold Rush, 99-107, 142
Goldwyn, Samuel, Jewish movie producer, 187-189
Great Basin, Utah, 92
Great Salt Lake, Utah, 92, 96
Guangdong Province, China, home of most early Chinese immigrants, 151
Guasti, Secundo, Italian-American vintner, 173
Guthrie, Woody (Woodrow Wilson), Okie singer and songwriter, 213, 214

H

Haas, Walter, family of, 185-187
Hallidie, Andrew S., English-American inventor of San Francisco cable cars, 128-130
Hastings' Cut-off, false shortcut for Donner Party, 114, 116
Hastings, Lansford, scout who misled Donner Party, 116
Hawkins, Augustus F., first California black elected to Congress, 149
Hawkins, Sir John, English privateer and relative of Francis Drake, 45
Hetch Hetchy Valley, in Sierra Nevada Mountains, 133
Higuerra, Josepha, wife of Robert Livermore, 127
Hispanics in California, 120-125
Hopkins, Mark, early California financier, 154
Humboldt River, much used route into California, 99, 114
Humboldt, see von Humboldt, Alexander
Huntington, C. P., early California financier, 154

I

J

K

L

M

T

U

W

Y

Z